The Cocktail Hour

The

COCKTAIL HOUR

APPETIZERS & DRINKS
FOR EVERY OCCASION

by *Helen Evans Brown*
and *Philip S. Brown*

THE WARD RITCHIE PRESS · *Los Angeles*

First paperback printing, 1972

COPYRIGHT 1958 BY HELEN EVANS BROWN
LIBRARY OF CONGRESS CATALOG CARD NUMBER 75-158492
ISBN 0378-01022-0
PRINTED IN THE UNITED STATES OF AMERICA
BY ANDERSON, RITCHIE & SIMON

The author wishes to thank SUNSET MAGAZINE *for permission to use in this book some of her recipes which have appeared in its pages.*

Introduction

Like it or not, the cocktail hour has come to stay. Most Americans *do* like it, for it is a welcome moment of relaxation after a busy day. Whether it is a quiet drink shared by husband or wife, or a gayer preprandial libation when guests are present, it is always pleasant. Even the large cocktail party has become a definite part of both business and social life in America. It is an ideal way to entertain a maximum crowd with a minimum of effort and expense. A cocktail party, strangely perhaps, doesn't necessarily mean that only cocktails are served. More and more Americans take highballs or sherry, champagne or even a non-alcoholic drink. But no matter what the size of the party or the type of drink being passed, some little something to nibble on is the order of the hour. That is the purpose of this book—to suggest a few things to serve and drinks to serve them with, or vice-versa.

Perhaps this book should be called "The Incomplete Book of Appetizers," for it is impossible to include more than a fraction of the things that fit into this category, which embraces anything with these prerequisites:

It should be easy to eat, preferably in the fingers;

It should be small—of bite—or at the most of two-bite size;

It should be well seasoned, even highly seasoned, unless wine is to be the *apéritif*;

But most of all, it should be dainty, delicious, and diverting.

Appetizers, the name I have chosen for these savory bits, is not a perfect one. Such a word, in English, does not exist. Hors d'oeuvre, our word through constant usage, comes closest to it, but that is really a first course, served at the table, like the Italian *antipasto*, Swedish *smörgasbord*, or Russian *zakousky*. Nor are they snacks, for in this country's vernacular a snack may be anything from an ounce bag of peanuts to a "yard-long" hot dog or a "mile-high" ice cream cone. They aren't really canapés, in the true sense of the word, for a canapé must be couched on toast or a similar base just as surely as the famed *smörrebrod* of Denmark is always built on buttered bread. They could be called tidbits or kickshaws (which word was what the English tongue did to the French *quelque chose*), but these savory little bites of goodness deserve a more important appelation. The French, as always when the problem is a gastronomic one, have the perfect solution. They call such a morsel a *bonne bouche*, or good mouthful. That last name tempted me, but I dare not use it for fear I would be accused of affectation or, and much worse, the title would frighten customers away.

And so I have settled on "appetizers," knowing full well that, in the original sense, they were meant to stimulate, not satisfy, the appetite. Most of the recipes in this book, if nibbled in discreet amounts, might whet the appetite, but any of them if eaten in sufficient quantity could well destroy it.

The host or hostess must decide what part these appetizers will play on any given occasion. If dinner, particularly one carefully planned and beautifully executed, is to follow after a drink or two, the appetizers should be few in quantity and variety. What cook wants a perfect pastry or *soufflé* untouched because the guests were stuffed with hot cheese do's? If, however, the guests are invited for cocktails only, the appetizers may—indeed should—be offered in much greater variety and quantity.

How many appetizers to allow each guest at a cocktail party is a question often asked and hard to answer. It depends, of course, on your guests. If they are the type who will drop in for a couple of rounds of drinks and then depart, four or five apiece should be enough. If, on the other hand, they are apt to arrive on the dot and remain until the lingering last, you'd better plan on as many as eight or ten for each person. They will need food for sustenance, and you'll want them to have it so the party won't get out of hand. Don't keep the food coming after they have outworn their welcome, though. Simply produce some black coffee and if they don't take *that* hint, cut off the supply of liquor.

How many drinks to allow each guest is another tough question to answer. You know best the thirst of your friends. A gallon of punch fills 40 punch cups. How many of those will each guest drink? Three? Thirteen? Take it from there. Likewise other drinks. A fifth of liquor will provide seventeen 1½-ounce drinks; a quart twenty-one of them. Thus, if the consumption is four drinks apiece, you'll need approximately a fifth for every four guests, a quart for every five. Get the idea? If champagne is the beverage, you'll get about five glasses from a bottle. Allowing three glasses a person, that will mean about two bottles for every three persons. Of course, you can allow less, or more. These figures are just a starting point. And don't forget that some people don't drink, so provide something non-alcoholic. There are some recipes in this book that fit that category.

The service at a cocktail party is another point to be considered. If it is a large one, by all means have the appetizers passed, either by professional help or by friends pressed into service. The drinks may be passed, or served from a bar, but again, you should have help. The host or hostess should always be free to circulate at such parties, so don't expect to mix the drinks or heat and pass the appetizers yourself.

If the party is a small intimate one, the host can and should mix the drinks himself, and the hostess should pass the hors d'oeuvre. If she is skillful, she can even heat them in the kitchen without being missed too much, but it is nicer to use some of the modern table appliances and do them before the guests. Or, of course, have help in the kitchen.

The appetizers, as I have said before, should be kept small. They also should be easy to eat. Do avoid fragile or drippy things that may ruin a guest's clothing or your rugs. The toothpick, more elegantly called the cocktail pick, is the hostess' best friend. However, be sure when using them that the appetizers have sufficient substance to stay on the pick. If in doubt, serve them in little bonbon cups or cases made with aluminum foil (see next paragraph). If dunks or spreads are served, I advise giving each guest a small plate and spreader. It is deadly to pass the things and have to wait while each guest eats his fill, and if you leave it to the guests to help themselves, chances are they won't. Actually, I think dunks and spreads should be skipped unless the party is a large one where the guests are standing anyway, and won't mind a buffet. Even then they should be limited to parties held outdoors or in a barn. Why spot the carpets?

The aluminum cases I spoke of above are easily made by cutting circles of heavy-duty aluminum foil and pressing them over the bottom of a shot glass or small bottle, to form little cups. More substantial ones, for baking tiny tart shells, may be made with triple layers of the foil, in the same way. And if you want your tart shells to be boat-shaped, like barquettes, press the foil over the bottom of an oval bottle or something else of the right shape. (When making tart shells, I slip the case back over the bottle bottom when forming the pastry over it, then bake them, pastry and foil together, on a cookie sheet, with their bottoms up.)

In this book you will find many recipes for drinks, as well as appetizers. My husband, Philip Brown, has chosen them with simplicity in mind. They require only the ingredients usually found in the home bar. You will find them at the bottoms of the pages, in no particular order, but they are well indexed.

As for the appetizers in this book, they do not pretend to be all new. Some are, at least as new as the day I concocted them, but I am well aware that talk of a new appetizer travels as fast as scandal, so even the latest ones may beat this book from the press. Some of the appetizers are old standbys but with, I hope, new twists. Still others are old—so old that, like the jokes that appear as new to every generation, they may be new to you. But new or not, I hope that they will add to your party fun, and that they will inspire you to create some of your very own.

HELEN EVANS BROWN

Pasadena, California.

1. *Teriyaki*

This is a great favorite in Hawaii and it has dozens of variations. Probably the simplest is this: Have a piece of boneless sirloin cut an inch thick. Slice this in ¼- to ½-inch slices, and marinate in a mixture of 1 part soy sauce, 1 part sherry, sake, or whiskey, and 1 part sesame or peanut oil. Weave on little bamboo sticks (available in Japanese stores and specialty shops) and broil over charcoal until done to your liking. Eat from the sticks. Grated ginger or garlic may be added to the marinade. If preferred, the meat may be cut in cubes and strung on skewers, alternating with stuffed green olives and chunks of pineapple.*

*Pork, chicken, fish, and game may be treated the same way—and also be called Teriyaki.

2. *Fondue Bourguignonne*

A wonderful appetizer for an informal party, this, not to be confused with a cheese fondue. For this one have a chafing dish or electric skillet with ½ pound of melted butter sizzling in it. Have a plate of raw tenderloin or sirloin of beef, cut in ¾- or 1-inch cubes. Give each guest a fondue or other long-handled fork, and let him spear his meat and cook it to the desired doneness in the hot butter. Have also a cold dunk, made by creaming butter with seasoning. The hot meat cubes are rolled in the cold butter before eating from the fork, or on small slices of French bread.*

*Here are some favorite seasonings to be added to ¼ pound of soft butter: (1) One large clove of pressed garlic. (2) Four mashed anchovies and a tablespoon of paprika. (3) 1 tablespoon each of minced chives and parsley. (4) 1 tablespoon of Worcestershire sauce and a dash of Tabasco.

3. *Charred Steak Squares*

Just as steak is an all-American favorite, so these steak squares are everyone's favorite appetizers. They are best done out-doors, over charcoal. Simply select a well-aged top sirloin or strip steak—one about 1½ inches thick is best for this—and broil it over a very hot fire, allowing the fat to drip and flare enough to char the outside. Keep the steak blood rare, and cut into 1-inch squares. Pop into a chafing dish with plenty of melted butter, sprinkle with salt and a grinding of pepper, and let the guests spear out their own and eat them as is, or put them on small pieces of bread. And if anyone wants well done steak, he can easily fork a piece and hold it over the fire until done to his liking.

EL PRESIDENTE: *Shake well with ice: 2 ounces of light rum, the juice of ¼ orange, and 2 dashes of grenadine. Strain into cocktail glass.*

4. *Kottbullar*

Swedish meat balls, these have a finer texture than ordinary meat balls because the meat is ground three times and the mixture beaten. Combine 1½ pounds of beef and ½ pound of pork, and grind 3 times, using the fine blade. Add 3 tablespoons of chopped onion sautéed in 2 tablespoons of butter, ½ cup of dried bread crumbs, 2½ teaspoons of salt, 1 cup of milk, some pepper, and 1 teaspoon of ground ginger. Beat, using an electric mixer if possible, until smooth and creamy. Chill, form in balls, and fry in butter, shaking the pan continuously to keep the meat balls round. Serve on toothpicks.

AKVAVIT: *This great Scandinavian "water of life" is always served neat and very cold. Keep the bottle in the refrigerator or freezer, and serve in little liqueur glasses. If the party is outside, keep the bottle buried in ice, or standing in a hollowed-out block of ice.*

5. Polpette

Italian meat balls, these. Combine 1 pound each of ground beef and veal with 2 cloves of garlic crushed to nothingness in 2 teaspoons of salt, ½ cup of grated Parmesan, ¼ cup of minced parsley, some fresh black pepper, ½ teaspoon of rosemary, ½ cup of bread crumbs, 2 tablespoons of red wine, and 2 eggs. Mix well, form in walnut-sized balls, roll in flour, and sauté in olive oil or at least *part* olive oil. Serve on toothpicks from a chafing dish, with or without Italian style tomato sauce.

MARTINI-ON-THE-ROCKS: *This is a popular way with martinis, perhaps because it eliminates the mixing glass. Put 2 or 3 ice cubes in a small old-fashioned glass, pour over gin and dry vermouth in your favorite proportions, add a twist of lemon peel, stir gently, and serve.*

6. Curried Chicken Meat Balls

Mix 2 pounds of ground raw chicken or turkey with ½ cup of grated onion, 1 tablespoon of curry powder, 1 egg, 2 teaspoons of salt, 2 teaspoons of lemon juice, and 2 tablespoons of crumbs. Form in balls, roll in flour, and sauté in butter. Serve in a chafing dish, in curry sauce, each ball impaled on a toothpick. Also have a bowl of freshly grated cocoanut mixed with a little chopped green chile and chopped raw apple, to dunk the balls in. Quick curry sauce: Sauté a crushed clove of garlic in 2 tablespoons of butter until soft; discard garlic. Add 1 tablespoon of curry powder (less if desired), 2 tablespoons of flour, and a cup of chicken stock. Cook until thick, then season with salt and pepper to taste, and 2 tablespoons of tomato catsup or a little lemon juice.

GUIDED MISSILE: *This high-powered cousin of the French '75 is made with rum instead of gin. In a highball glass put ½ ounce of lemon juice, sugar to taste, and 2 ounces of light rum. Add plenty of ice cubes, fill to the top with chilled Champagne, and stir.*

7. Meat Balls With Sour Cream Sauce

One of the most satisfactory of appetizers, these may be made ahead, frozen, and reheated in various sauces. Combine 1 pound of ground beef, 1 egg, and 1 slice of bread moistened with 1 tablespoon of milk. Season with a teaspoon of salt and some pepper. Form in small balls and sauté gently in butter. Serve with sour cream sauce: Sauté a small chopped onion in 2 tablespoons of butter until wilted. Stir in a tablespoon of flour, ½ teaspoon of salt, a tablespoon of paprika, and ¼ cup of beef stock or bouillon. When thick and hot, add a cup of sour cream and heat but do not cook.*

*These meat balls may be varied by tucking cubes of cheese, or small stuffed olives, or rolled anchovies in their centers when forming, or by mixing chopped sautéed onions or any favorite seasoning with the meat.

8. *Chinese Meat Balls*

My Chinese isn't very good, but I've been told these are called *jar yook yun*. Could be, but they are good in English, too. Mix together a pound of lean ground pork and a cup of chopped water chestnuts. Add a teaspoon of salt, a crushed clove of garlic, a tablespoon of soy sauce, a teaspoon of cornstarch, 1 egg, and ¼ cup of minced green onions. Form in small balls, roll in cornstarch, and sauté in oil. Serve on toothpicks in a chafing dish, along with pineapple cubes, also on toothpicks, and the following sauce: 1 cup of pineapple juice, 1 tablespoon of soy sauce, 1 tablespoon of grated ginger, 2 tablespoons of green pepper slivers, 2 tablespoons of vinegar, and 1 tablespoon of cornstarch moistened in ¼ cup of stock. Cook until clear.

LIBERTY: *Shake well with ice: 2 ounces of applejack, 1 ounce of light rum, and a little sugar or simple syrup. Strain into a cocktail glass.*

9. *Grecian Meat Balls, Avgolemono*

Avgolemono may be Greek to you, but you'll find it's a delicious lemon sauce in which to dip Grecian—or any other —meat balls. Make the meat balls with 1 pound of ground beef or lamb, ½ cup of chopped onion, ½ cup of pine nuts, 1 egg, 2 tablespoons each of minced parsley and mint, 1 teaspoon of salt, and a dash of pepper. Form in balls and sauté in butter. The sauce: Beat 1 whole egg and 2 egg yolks with 3 tablespoons of lemon juice. Gradually beat in a cup of hot well-seasoned meat broth or consommé. Do not cook further, or the sauce will curdle.*

*A stabler method is to make a roux of 2 tablespoons each of butter and flour, add the stock and lemon juice, and 1 egg yolk.

10. *Rumaki*

This has been popular for several years, but it still surprises—and delights—some people, so I dare not skip it. Cut chicken livers in halves and dip quickly in soy sauce. Slice canned water chestnuts in 3 pieces. Split bacon slices lengthwise (a trick I stole from Ruth Bateman, food writer, and everybody's honey). Sandwich a piece of chicken liver between two slices of water chestnut, wind in a long piece of bacon, fasten with a pick, and put on a rack in a 400° oven. Bake until the bacon is crisp and brown.*

*These may be broiled or fried, but if they are, they will have to be turned.

11. *Lobster With Water Chestnuts*

This is a version of rumaki, and a good one. Substitute good-size chunks of tail meat from a lightly cooked lobster for the chicken livers, and use only 1 slice of water chestnut. Proceed as for rumaki. Or use shrimps in place of the lobster.*

*Another variation on this theme is to include a chunk of pineapple along with the lobster or shrimp.

12. *Bacon Brazil Nuts*

Wrap shelled Brazil nuts in a split slice of bacon, fasten with a pick, and cook in a 375° oven until the bacon is crisp. If that's too simple, roll the nut in curry powder first.

RUM FRAPPÉ: *Place a scoop of orange or lemon sherbet in a Champagne glass. Cover with rum, as desired, stir, and serve.*

13. *Tidbits in Bacon*

Parboil sweetbreads in acidulated water for 10 minutes. Chill, clean, and cut in walnut-sized pieces. Wrap in split slices of bacon, fasten with toothpicks, and broil until the bacon is crisp. If you like the idea, marinate the sweetbreads in sherry before you bacon-wrap them. Shad roe and calves brains, or liver, or kidneys, and other tidbits can be prepared and cooked in the same way, though the roe is improved by dipping in lemon juice before wrapping.

OLD-FASHIONED: *Muddle a lump of sugar, 2 dashes of bitters, and a splash of charged water in an old-fashioned glass. Add a couple of ice cubes, 2 or 3 ounces of Bourbon, and a twist of lemon. Stir just to mix. If you're a true old-fashioned lover, you'll skip the tutti-frutti garnish.*

14. *Angelenos*

This is a twist on that old favorite, Angels on Horseback—oysters wrapped in bacon and broiled. The difference here is that the oyster is first circled with an anchovy fillet (a split one if the oyster is small), then wound with bacon (again, a split slice if . . .), and the bacon secured with a toothpick. Before serving, put on a rack in a baking pan, and cook in a 375° or 400° oven until the bacon is crisp. (This saves turning and watching; you can broil if you prefer to work harder.)*

Fried oysters: Egg and crumb them, fry in butter until golden on both sides, impale on picks or couch on toast, and serve with tartare sauce.

15. *Char Siu*

This Chinese roast pork may be served hot, warm, or cold. Marinate a pork tenderloin in a mixture of ½ cup of soy sauce, ½ cup of Bourbon whiskey, 3 tablespoons of honey, and a crushed clove of garlic. Bake at 300° for 1½ hours. Serve sliced thin, and impale on picks, if you wish, though fingers do nicely.

MINT TULIP: *(Non-alcoholic) Bruise a bunch of fresh mint leaves in ½ cup of water; add 2 cans of frozen concentrated lemonade and let stand 30 minutes. Add 3 pints of ginger ale, mix, and pour over ice in a punch bowl.*

16. *Pig in a Poke*

The pig is a tiny pork sausage, the poke a prune with the pit removed. Select plump prunes, the tender kind that are good eaten raw. Remove the pits, replace them with partially-cooked sausages or little balls of sausage meat. Wrap in a slice of bacon—halved and then split—fasten with a toothpick, and bake until the bacon is very crisp.

SHANDYGAFF: *A good rugged cooler with years of experience. A tall glass is half filled with chilled ale, then filled to the top with chilled ginger ale.*

17. *Chick in a Poke*

This is a variation on the pig in a poke (page 16). Stuff the prunes with quarters of chicken livers that have been lightly sautéed in butter. Add a sliver of water chestnut if you like the idea—I do. Wrap in bacon and proceed as before. Cubes of cooked ham, duck, goose, and pork are all good fixed this way, too. So are cubes of sharp Cheddar cheese, or Roquefort. Play around with the idea and you'll probably come up with many more.

SCOTCH MIST: *Fill an old-fashioned glass with shaved ice. Pour in Scotch whisky as desired. Add a twist of lemon peel.*

18. *Virginia Ham Biscuits*

This is as old as Southern hospitality, but it is still unexcelled. The ham must be of the best, and sliced wafer thin. The biscuits, too, must be superlative—either beaten biscuits or tiny rich baking powder biscuits. I find that the packaged ready-to-bake kind do nicely; I pull each one into an oval, cut 2 2½-inch rounds from it, and then mix all the scraps together and roll them to get 24 small biscuits in all. Bake at 500° for 8 minutes, split, butter, and sandwich the ham between the halves at once. Serve hot, do.

COLLINS: *A Collins may be made with gin, vodka, rum, whiskey, applejack, or brandy. Pour 2 or 3 ounces of liquor over ice in a tall glass, add ½ ounce of lemon juice and sugar to taste, and fill up with charged water. Stir, garnish with a twist of lemon peel, and serve.*

19. *Josefinas*

These are lusty, gusty, inexpensive, and easy. Slice French rolls or French bread flutes—what you want are miniature slices of bread with the crusts on. Spread them with ½ pound of soft butter, well mixed with 1 cup of chopped canned green chiles and a pressed clove of garlic (optional). Top with a mixture of ½ pound of shredded Jack or Cheddar cheese that has been mixed with 1 cup of mayonnaise (not salad dressing). Spread topping clear to the edges, using a good rounded teaspoon for each piece. Broil until brown and puffy, and serve hot. This makes about 5 dozen.

GOLDEN FIZZ: *Shake well with ice: 3 ounces of dry gin, the juice of ½ lime and ½ lemon, 1 egg yolk, and sugar to taste. Strain into a highball glass and fill up with charged water.*

20. *Panitas*

These, dreamed up by Jessica McLachlin Greengard of Wine Institute fame, were the inspiration for *Josefinas*. Slice French bread and cut in halves or quarters. Spread it liberally with a mixture of 1 cup of mayonnaise, 1 cup of grated Cheddar cheese, and 1 cup of finely minced green onions. Broil until billowy brown.

SILVER FIZZ: *Shake well with ice: 3 ounces of dry gin, the juice of ½ lemon and ½ lime, 1 egg white, and sugar to taste. Strain into a highball glass and fill up with charged water.*

21. *Inflated Crackers*

Actually, it's the topping on these that inflates when they are toasted under the broiler. You start with cooked shrimp or crab meat or lobster. Minced clams or smoked oysters are good, too, and so are ham or sardines or cooked chicken livers. Chop whatever you have, mix ¾ cup of it with ½ cup of mayonnaise and a stiffly beaten egg white, season with whatever you like: curry with the shellfish, chives with the clams, dill or tarragon with the chicken livers, and salt with all of them. Pile on crackers, slip under the broiler, and cook until brown and inflated.

WHITE WINE COBBLER: *Fill a tumbler ⅔ full of cracked ice. Add ½ teaspoon of sugar and a teaspoon of lemon juice. Fill with dry white wine (or Rhine wine), stir slightly, and serve with a twist of lemon peel and a sprig of mint.*

22. *Finnan Haddie Toasts*

Combine a cup of cooked flaked finnan haddie with a sauce made of 2 tablespoons each of butter and flour, and ⅔ cup of cream. Season to taste, and when cold, spread on toast rounds. Sprinkle with crumbs, dot with a tiny bead of butter, and bake or broil until brown.*

*This same mixture, or one using equal amounts of fish and sauce, is good in tiny tart shells.

23. *Hamburg Toasts*

These are the only hamburgers I really like. Grind lean rump steak just before using. Slice French rolls or flutes and toast on one side. Spread the other side with butter and then with the beef. Sprinkle with salt and pepper, and broil just enough to heat up the meat. Serve at once. You can trick these up with herbs or cheese or relish, but don't. It's their simplicity that gives them such winning ways.

BRONX COCKTAIL: *Stir well with ice: 2 ounces of dry gin, ½ ounce of dry vermouth, and the juice of ¼ orange. Strain into cocktail glass.*

24. *Cheese & Bacon Do's*

What's a "do"? Anything you want to make it. These I made by cutting slices of bread in 1-inch squares, toasting one side or not, and spreading with butter highly seasoned with garlic (1 stick of butter to a large pressed clove of garlic). On top of this I spread a mixture of ½ pound of grated Cheddar to 2 very well beaten eggs. Next comes an inch of sliced bacon, and the "do" is put under the broiler until puffily brown.*

*This can be varied by adding a little orégano or chili powder, or even curry, to the cheese and egg mixture.

25. *Garlic Shrimps*

Anyone who likes shrimps will like these. Select raw jumbo shrimps and, if serving at an indoor party, remove shells and sand veins. If serving outdoors, simply split shells up the back with scissors, and rinse out sand veins. Marinate in equal parts of soy sauce, peanut oil, and sherry, Cognac or whiskey, with 2 crushed cloves of garlic for an hour or two. Drain and broil over charcoal or in the oven for 4 or 5 minutes on each side. Serve shelled ones on toothpicks, others with hot towels or finger bowls. Grated ginger can be added to this marinade, with gratifying results.*

*Variations: Marinate in equal parts of olive oil and vermouth; or white wine and butter, seasoned with tarragon; or in olive oil, lemon juice, parsley and garlic.

26. *Mushrooms With Oysters (Hot)*

Prepare mushrooms as in recipe for pâté-stuffed mushrooms. Put a drained oyster in each mushroom, sprinkle with a little lemon juice, and top with a mixture of ½ cup of cracker crumbs, ½ cup of butter, a tablespoon each of minced parsley and chives. Broil until brown, and serve in foil cups. If preferred, the crumbs may be omitted and the oyster topped with an inch of sliced bacon before broiling.*

*A variation is to use half a sautéed chicken liver or a cooked shrimp in place of the oyster.

27. Shrimps and Things in Cognac

Shell a pound of green shrimps, medium or large, and sauté them in ½ cup (1 bar) of butter for 4 minutes. Season with salt and pepper. Add 2 jiggers of Cognac, flame, and serve at once on picks or small rounds of toast. For variation on this, add tarragon or shallots to the shrimps. Cubes of raw turkey or chicken breast, or pieces of lobster tail may be treated the same way—so may mushrooms and chicken livers.

QUARTERDECK COCKTAIL: *Shake well with ice: 1 dash of bitters, 2 ounces of Jamaica rum, 1 ounce of dry sherry, 1 ounce of Scotch, and ½ teaspoon of sugar. Strain into a cocktail glass.*

28. Codfish Balls, 1927

These were my favorites way back when cocktails were made with bathtub gin and tasted like varnish. Soak a pound of salt codfish in water to cover for 2 hours. Drain, cover with fresh water, and bring to a boil. Drain and pull into pieces. Combine with 2 cups of riced potatoes (packed in cup) and 4 very well beaten eggs. Beat thoroughly, and drop by teaspoons into hot deep fat at 380°. Fry brown, drain, and serve very hot on picks. Small gherkins are good with these, and some people like catsup, too, though goodness knows why.

BATHTUB GIN: *Mix together in a clean bathtub, 5 gallons of grain alcohol, 8 gallons of distilled water, 8 ounces of glycerine, and essence of juniper to taste. Blend well, sampling occasionally, and bottle in gallon containers.*

29. *Chinese Fried Shrimps*

There are many different ways to do this most popular of shrimp dishes. In each case the shrimps (large or jumbos, please) are shelled, but the shell end of the tail is left on. The black vein may be removed or not, as you like. I like. The shrimps are then dipped in fritter batter and fried in deep fat at 370° until nicely browned. Or dip in flour and then in beaten egg, in that order. Or in egg and cracker crumbs. If you want a more definite recipe, here: 2 eggs, 1 cup of water, 1 cup of flour, 2 tablespoons of cornstarch, ¼ cup of corn meal, ¾ cup of milk, ½ teaspoon of salt, ½ teaspoon of baking powder. If a dip for the cooked shrimps is desired, have catsup and hot prepared mustard, in the Chinese manner.*

*Tempura, *the Japanese fritter, is much the same, but the sauce is different. Try ¼ cup each of sherry and shoyu, 1 teaspoon of sugar, and 1 tablespoon of grated ginger.*

30. Snails in Mushrooms

Make snail butter by creaming ½ pound of butter with ½ cup of finely minced parsley and 2 large garlic cloves, mashed to nothing or put through a garlic press. Rinse canned snails with water or—in the French manner—with wine. Clean mushroom caps of uniform size, preferably about 1½ inches in diameter. Remove stems and put a little butter in each cap. Put a snail (or a shrimp, if you're not a lover of *les escargots*) in each cap, and cover with more of the butter. Put caps in little aluminum bonbon cases, if you can find them; if not, make some by pressing circles of heavy-duty aluminum foil over the bottom of a shot glass or similar small round object. This will keep the juices from spilling. Bake in a 425° oven for about 10 minutes. Serve at once, in the foil cases. Have small pieces of crusty bread handy, too.

EMPRESS *(or* Queen's Peg*): Put a piece of ice in a large wine glass. Add 2 ounces of dry gin, and fill up with chilled Champagne.*

31. *Frogs' Legs Provençale*

Surprising, perhaps, for an appetizer, but very good. Select medium-sized frogs' legs and separate. Dip them in milk, dust thoroughly with flour, and sauté quickly in olive oil to which 3 or 4 crushed cloves of garlic have been added. This can be done before the guests, in a chafing dish or electric skillet. When the legs are beautifully browned, discard garlic, drain off surplus oil, and sprinkle the legs with finely minced parsley. These are finger food, so provide hot fingertip towels or finger bowls and napkins.

IMPERIAL *(or* King's Peg*): Put a piece of ice in a large wine glass. Add 2 ounces of Cognac, and fill up with chilled Champagne.*

32. *Oysters and Sausages*

We had this in Cognac, the home of the world's finest brandy. It makes an interesting appetizer, as the hot crispy pork sausages are a perfect partner for the iced oysters on the half shell. And that is the recipe!

BLOCKBUSTER *(for 8): Shake gently with ice: 10 ounces of Cognac, 10 ounces of applejack, 4 teaspoons of grenadine and 3 tablespoons of lemon juice. Strain into cocktail glasses.*

33. Fruits With Curry Sauce

Exotic, this, and just a bit drippy, so keep the group small enough to sit around the chafing dish. The curry sauce is kept hot in that. The fruits—cubes of pineapple, apple, banana, papaya, mango, orange, or what-you-will—are impaled on long sticks. (The applicator sticks from the druggist, or the split bamboo sticks from Japan-town will do). Each guest dips the fruit in the curry sauce, then rolls it in a dish of chopped salted almonds or grated cocoanut. The sauce: Sauté a small finely-grated onion in 3 tablespoons of butter. Add 3 tablespoons of flour, 2 tablespoons of curry powder, 1 cup of chicken broth, and 2 teaspoons of lemon juice. Add salt to taste and more curry if needed. Cook until smooth and thick.

GIMLET: *Shake well with ice: 3 ounces of dry gin and 1 ounce of lime juice. Strain into large cocktail glass and add a splash of charged water.*

34. Fried Chicken Gizzards

This is a thrift special, as you know if you've ever patronized a market where chicken parts are sold. Cover them with water, toss in a couple of slices of onion and an herb bouquet, and simmer slowly until very tender. Drain (save that stock, it's good!) and cut each gizzard in half. Roll in flour, then dip in slightly beaten egg and seasoned crumbs, and fry in deep fat (370°) until crisply brown. These are most easily eaten from picks and, strangely, they are good cold as well as hot.*

*"Seasoned crumbs" is the cue to variety—to them you can add curry powder, chili powder, or herbs.

35. *Raclette*

This is a specialty of the Canton du Valais, in Switzerland. A sort of fondue, it is simplicity itself. Serve it when you're cooking out-of-doors, or when there's a fire in the fireplace. Here's why: Select a large piece of cheese, any kind that melts well. As we cannot find the *fromage du pays* of Switzerland, a well-aged Cheddar is probably the best choice. Put it so close to the fire that the cut surface will melt. Have hot plates and butter spreaders handy—also a large dull-bladed knife. As the cheese melts, scrape a molten layer onto one of the guests' plates. Have also crusty bread, radishes, raw onions, and a pepper mill, so each guest can make his own feast. The Swiss serve potatoes "en chemise" and the white wine of the region —that way, it's a meal!

NEUCHÂTEL: *The white wines of the Neu-châtel region of Switzerland are light and rather thin, but lively and refreshing. Serve a chilled Domaine de Champreveyres with this raclette, for a perfect combination.*

36. *Cheese Balls*

Impressive these, but no work at all unless you are allergic to deep-fat frying. With modern automatic fryers, there's really nothing to that, either. Beat 2 large egg whites stiff. Combine with 1½ cups of grated Cheddar, 2 teaspoons of flour, ½ teaspoon of salt, and a dash of cayenne. Roll in marble-sized balls, then in fine cracker meal, and fry in deep fat at 375°. Drain on paper towels and serve pronto. These may be frozen before or after frying. In the latter case, heat in a 350° oven for 10 minutes if thawed, 15 minutes if frozen.

SCREWDRIVER: *Pour over ice, in a 6-ounce glass, 2 ounces of vodka. Fill with orange juice and stir lightly.*

37. Carnitas

"Little meats" is the translation of this recipe of Elena's—that wonderful cook and wonderful person. It, along with many others, is in *Elena's Secrets of Mexican Cooking*. Cut lean pork into 1-inch cubes and sprinkle with salt and pepper. Bake in a shallow pan in a 300° oven for 1½ to 2 hours, stirring and pouring off the surplus fat as it accumulates. When tender, brown, and crispy but *not* dried out, serve on picks or, as Elena does, with toasted tortilla wedges and guacamole. Sensational!

CUBA LIBRE: *Pour 2 ounces of any rum over ice in a tall glass. Fill with cola and squeeze in ½ lime.*

38. *Chinese Stuffed Mushrooms*

A warning on these: Don't have too many because they will all be devoured, and they are filling enough to spoil appetites for dinner. Select a pound of uniform-sized mushroom caps— about 1½ inches is a good size. Clean and remove stems. Put them in a covered saucepan with a tablespoon of butter and 2 of broth, and simmer 3 minutes. Make a filling with ½ pound of cooked ground pork, 3 chopped green onions, 4 minced water chestnuts, 2 teaspoons of soy sauce, a tablespoon of oil, a dash of cayenne, and a teaspoon of grated green or candied ginger (the latter rinsed of its sugar). Blend well, stuff mushroom caps, dip them upside-down in sesame seeds. Put in a pan with the juices in which the mushrooms cooked, and bake in a 375° oven until hot and the sesame seeds lightly browned. Put in bonbon or small foil cups for easier serving.

BLOODY MARY: *(No. 2): Shake well with ice: 2 ounces of vodka, 4 ounces of tomato juice, ½ ounce of lemon juice, and a dash of Worcestershire sauce. Strain into a cold glass. Salt and pepper may be added, if you like.*

39. *Mushrooms à la Virginia Tilton*

This recipe I have purloined from *The Virginia City Cook Book*, which my husband and I wrote along with famed writers Katharine Best and Katharine Hillyer, and famed artist Harry Diamond. Select 1 pound of uniform mushrooms about 1½ inches in diameter, if possible. Remove stems, and sauté caps in 3 tablespoons of butter for 4 minutes. Remove. In same pan put another tablespoon of butter, a cup of chicken livers, and 2 tablespoons of finely minced shallots. Sauté until the livers lose their color. Chop fine, season with salt and pepper, and ¼ teaspoon of dried tarragon. Fill the mushroom caps with this and top each with the tiniest piece of anchovy filet—not more than ¼-inch. This gives that fascinating flavor fillip. Serve hot or cold.*

*Chopped raw mushrooms, mixed with liver pâté or Roquefort cheese, and formed in balls are good. Roll them in minced chives or parsley or nuts.

40. *Meat Balls en Croûte*

Make 1-inch meat balls according to any of the recipes in this book. Roll out rich pastry and cut in 2-inch circles; put a meat ball on one, cover with another, press edges tightly together, and glaze the top with an egg yolk beaten with a tablespoon of milk. Bake in a 400° oven until a lovely amber.*

**Vary these by making balls of soft Cheddar or other cheese, or of ground ham or chicken liver mixed with enough mayonnaise to bind.*

41. *Terrific Tarts*

Make tiny tart shells (see Index). In the bottom of each put a spoonful of hot cooked puréed spinach, well seasoned. Next put a smoked oyster (or a shrimp), and fill the tart with Mornay sauce. Sprinkle with grated cheese and broil until brown. A simple Mornay sauce is made by adding ¼ cup each of grated Swiss and Gruyère cheese to a cup of white sauce.

BRANDY SMASH: *In an old-fashioned glass put ½ teaspoon of fine sugar, 2 sprigs of fresh mint, and a few drops of water. Crush the mint with a muddler and half-fill the glass with shaved ice. Pour in 2 or 3 ounces of brandy and, if wanted, a splash of charged water. Decorate with mint.*

42. *Bouchées de Tomate*

These take a bit of patience, but they're worth it. Cut 1½-inch rounds from French bread sliced ¼-inch thick. Spread sparsely with mayonnaise, then top with a slice of cherry (or egg) tomato. That's where the patience comes in—you'll need a razor-sharp knife to slice those flavorsome little red tomatoes. Now mix together ¼ cup each of finely chopped green onion and green pepper, add ½ cup of mayonnaise, ½ cup of grated Cheddar, and ¼ teaspoon of salt. Cover tomato with this mixture, top with a half-inch square of sliced bacon, and broil until the bacon is crisp. Let cool a minute or two (the tomatoes keep them *very* hot!) then pop the whole canapé into the mouth. If you try it in two bites there just may be a catastrophe.

FOG CUTTER: *Shake well with ice: 2 ounces of light rum, 1½ ounces of brandy, 1 ounce of gin, 1½ ounces of orange juice, 1½ ounces of lemon juice, and ½ ounce of simple syrup. Pour into a tall glass with the ice, and float sherry on top. Serve with straws.*

43. *Chinese Egg Rolls*

These may be made with paper-thin pancakes, or crêpes (see Index), but I like them better when done this way. Mix equal parts of flour and water, and, using a small brush, paint on a lightly greased, not-too-hot griddle, in a 5-inch square. Stroke one way and then the other to fill up any holes. Remove as soon as dry. It will be thin as rice paper. Put a roll of filling (see next page) on one side, turn over the edges, and roll up like a bed roll, pasting the edges together with some of the flour and water. Before serving, fry in shallow or deep fat (at 370°) until bubbly brown. Cut in pieces for serving on toothpicks or in bonbon cases.

BRANDY TODDY: *Dissolve 1 lump of sugar in a tumbler with a little water, and add 4 ounces of brandy and a twist of lemon peel. Fill with boiling water, stir and serve.*

44. *Fillings for Egg Rolls*

Crab Filling: Combine a pound of crab meat with a pound of ground fresh pork, ½ cup of minced green onions, ½ cup of minced water chestnuts, a tablespoon of soy sauce, and a beaten egg yolk.

Chicken Filling: Combine a pound of ground raw chicken, ½ pound of ground Virginia ham, ½ cup of chopped water chestnuts, 1 tablespoon of soy sauce, a beaten egg yolk, and 2 teaspoons of grated fresh or candied ginger.

Mushroom Filling: Combine ½ pound each of ground pork and ham (or shrimps), ¼ cup of minced green onions, 1 cup of chopped bean sprouts, ¼ cup of minced water chestnuts, ½ pound of chopped mushrooms (cooked in 3 tablespoons of oil), 2 teaspoons of cornstarch, and a tablespoon of soy sauce.

THE HUNTRESS: *Shake well with ice: 2 ounces of vodka, ½ ounce of Jamaica rum, the juice of ½ lime, and sugar to taste. Strain into a cocktail glass.*

45. *Bagels With Lox*

An old favorite Jewish snack, bagels with cream cheese and lox (smoked salmon) is sensational as an appetizer when made in miniature. They are fun to make, but if that isn't your idea of fun, get the regular-sized ones, slice them into small rounds (if you want the slices even, you'll have a few wedges left over, but so what?). Toast the slices or not, as you please (I don't), spread with softened cream cheese, and top with a thin slice of lox, and serve. The recipe for miniature bagels is on the next page.*

*Another Jewish favorite, gefillte fish, *may be heated, impaled on toothpicks and dunked in a sour cream and horseradish sauce.*

46. *Baby Bagels*

I'm cheating on this recipe and using a hot roll mix. Add a tablespoon of sugar to the mix and follow the directions on the package. After the first rising, turn out on a floured board and knead for 5 minutes or until elastic. Cover and let stand for 15 minutes, then roll ¼-inch thick and cut in rounds of 1¼ to 1½ inches. Cut holes in the middle with a tiny cutter if you want to simulate the adult size, but it isn't necessary. Drop bagels, a few at a time, in a large pot of boiling water. They will rise to the surface quickly. Lift them from the water with a slotted spoon and shake off surplus water. Arrange on greased cookie sheets and bake in a 400° oven for 10 minutes, or until nicely browned. Split and spread with the cream cheese and lox, then put together again, making a sandwich.*

*And for an easy one, wrap paper-thin slices of pastrami around fingers of Kosher dill pickles, or make a sandwich of slices of pickle with a filling of smoked fish.

47. Midget Crêpes

These are minute and they really take only a minute—or three—to make. And such possibilities they have. Make a thin crêpe batter with 2 eggs, 1 cup each of flour and milk, 1 tablespoon of Cognac, 1 tablespoon of melted butter, ½ teaspoon of salt. Heat a Swedish pancake pan (Svensk Plette pan) and butter it. Remove from heat and pour 1 teaspoonful of batter in one depression; tip so that it flows evenly over the entire surface. Continue until all 7 compartments are filled, then return to the heat and cook just long enough to brown the bottoms. Do not brown other sides. Spread unbaked sides with any savory filling and roll, or put a spoonful of filling on one half, and fold other half over it. Serve hot. (They may be reheated in a moderate oven for a few minutes.) These really create a sensation.*

*Use these tiny crêpes instead of blinis, if you wish. They're tops with caviar!

48. *Blinis*

These will be the talk of the town. You can use the recipe for midget crêpes (on preceding page) for these, but they won't be as authentic as if made with buckwheat. And, because buckwheat flour is hard to find and buckwheat pancake mix is on every grocer's shelf, I have concocted a recipe using that. Soften ½ cake of yeast in ¼ cup of warm water. Beat together 1 cup of buckwheat mix, 1 cup of milk, 1 egg, 1 tablespoon of melted butter, and the yeast mixture. Let rise in a warm place for an hour, then cook as for midget crêpes, using ½ tablespoon for each cake, or make into thin pancakes in a 3- or 4-inch frying pan. Serve hot with melted butter, iced caviar, and sour cream, or with smoked fish and sour cream, or with hard-boiled eggs that have been chopped and mixed with melted butter.

VODKA: *Very well chilled vodka served in liqueur glasses makes a fine preprandial libation. Put the bottle in your freezer for several hours beforehand. Or serve it "on the rocks": Pour 2 or 3 ounces of vodka over ice in an old-fashioned glass, top with a twist of lemon, and relax.*

49. *Waffled Treats*

Simple, these, and delectable. Make thin sandwiches of almost anything—cheese, pâté, ham, turkey, shrimp paste, or use a combination of meat and cheese, or two kinds of meat such as chicken and tongue. Brush both outsides of the sandwich with melted butter, and cook in a medium-hot waffle iron until nicely browned and "waffled." Trim crusts, cut in quarters, and serve hot. (These reheat nicely in the oven.)*

**Enrich this idea, if you must, by dipping the buttered sandwiches into egg and milk before cooking in the waffle iron.*

50. *Gougère*

I suppose it's sheer heresy to serve anything but a fine Burgundy with this lusty Burgundian cheese creation, but when made in miniature size and served piping hot, these are good with any beverage. Make a choux paste (see index for *petits choux*) and to it add ½ cup of very finely diced Swiss cheese. Drop by spoonfuls on cookie sheets and sprinkle with more finely diced Swiss cheese—about ¾ cup. Bake at 350° for 30 minutes and serve at once. These may be made ahead of time and refrigerated, or kept in a cool place until baking time. I find a kitchen timer a great help if I'm baking after guests have arrived.

FINE À L'EAU: *A Cognac highball is all this is, and very refreshing. Just add water or soda to Cognac, with or without ice, and sip away. Unless you want to pay through the nose for dubious whiskey, this is the best "American type" drink to order in France.*

51. *Croque-Monsieur*

This is a favorite Parisian *"snack,"* and don't think that isn't just what they now call it, though it used to be considered "une petite entrée." Make sandwiches with buttered white bread (*pain du mie*), sliced Swiss cheese, and sliced ham. Dip in a mixture of 1 beaten egg to each ¼ cup of milk, then fry in butter until brown on both sides. Cut in quarters and serve at once. At an informal gathering, do these in your electric skillet or in the electric grill, right in the living room or on the patio where the guests are sipping.*

*Croque-Madame, you may be interested to know, is the same thing except that chicken is substituted for the ham. More ladylike?

52. Philip's Special

Originally this was just a husky sandwich contrived by my husband after a successful raid of the refrigerator. Cut down to a less formidable size, it makes a fine appetizer. Slice a good Italian salami rather thin. Slice bread and cut in rounds the size of the salami. Do the same with Jack cheese. Butter the bread, make sandwiches with a slice each of the cheese and the salami, butter the outsides and cook on the griddle, or toast, or dip in batter and fry. Anyway they are good.

OAKLEY'S DREAM: *Dissolve a teaspoon of honey in a little boiling water. Pour into a shaker with a teaspoon of cream and 3 or 4 ounces of rum. Shake well with ice and strain into a cocktail glass. This may also be dreamed with gin, brandy, whiskey, or applejack.*

53. Miniature Monte Carlos

Make sandwiches of sliced boiled tongue and Swiss or Jack cheese. Trim crusts, dip in a mixture of 1 cup of milk, 2 eggs, ½ teaspoon of salt, and a little pepper, and fry in butter on both sides. Cut in quarters for immediate serving. Use turkey breast instead of tongue for a *Monte Cristo*, or make up and name your own combinations.

STRAWBERRY WINE BOWL: *Wash and slice a quart of ripe strawberries, and sprinkle with ¼ cup of sugar. Add 4 bottles of Riesling and 1 bottle of red Burgundy. Let the mixture stand in the refrigerator for an hour or more, then pour it over a block of ice and add 2 bottles of Champagne. This is delightful for a spring garden party.*

54. Miniature Oyster Loaves

In the days when it was possible to buy tiny Olympia oysters without floating a loan, I used them for this conceit. Now I cut larger oysters in halves or quarters. But first slice the tops from tiny rolls and scoop out the crumbs. Brush the cut surfaces with melted butter and toast in a 400° oven until lightly browned. Egg and crumb oysters and fry them crisp in deep fat. Cut them to fit the rolls, put a piece in each, drizzle on a drop or two of hot seasoned cream, replace tops on rolls, and serve hot.

GIN FIZZ: *Shake well with ice: 3 ounces of dry gin, the juice of ½ lemon and ½ lime, and sugar to taste. Strain into a highball glass and fill up with charged water.*

55. Croquettes

Like fritters, any kind of a croquette if small enough to pop into the mouth all at once, makes a superb appetizer. Basically, they are made the same way: Combine 2 cups of chopped whatever-you-choose, 1 cup of heavy cream sauce (1 cup of milk, 1/4 cup each of butter and flour), 1 egg yolk, and the seasonings of your choice. Chill, form in tiny croquettes or balls, roll in beaten egg and then in crumbs, and fry in deep fat at 390° until brown. Drain and serve on picks. Favorite croquettes are crab, shrimp, chicken, salmon, cheese and lobster.*

*Vary the seasonings in croquettes. Try curry or chili powder, dill, tarragon, chives, or a mixture of herbs.

56. *Fritters*

If I gave recipes for every kind of fritter that makes a good appetizer, there wouldn't be anything else in this book. So, except for a hint or two of what can be frittered, I leave this entirely to your imagination. Oysters, clams, anchovies, cooked sweetbreads, brains, liver, kidneys, roe, chicken livers, and any tasty tidbits are dipped in batter and fried crisp in deep fat at 370°. Batter: Beat together 1 cup of flour, 1 cup of milk, 2 egg yolks, 2 tablespoons of melted butter, 1 jigger of Cognac, and ½ teaspoon of salt. Let stand for an hour, then fold in 2 stiffly beaten egg whites.

BIG APPLE: *Stir well with ice: 2 ounces of applejack, 1 ounce of Cognac, 1 ounce of gin, and 2 ounces of sweet cider. Strain into cocktail glass.*

57. Diminutive Pizzas

I hesitate to include this recipe because such awful things have been done to pizzas (including calling them "pizza pies") that they have lost their charm for many of us. Still . . . . Use a hot roll dough, and after its first rising roll it thin and cut in 2½-inch circles. Put them on pans greased with garlic olive oil, and brush a little more of the oil on top. Now vary the toppings: On some have a thin slice of fresh tomato sprinkled with oregano; put a cross of anchovy fillets on this and a bit of grated cheese. Cover some with sliced Italian sausage, some with sliced sautéed mushrooms, some with sardines. These may be sauced or not, cheesed or not, garnished or not. The idea is to have them varied and savory. Another drizzle of the olive oil and, without further rising, a sojourn in a 375° oven until brown around the edges. Serve at once.

MAMIE TAYLOR: *Squeeze ¼ lemon or ½ lime into a highball glass, add ice cubes and 3 ounces of gin or Scotch whisky, and fill with cold ginger ale. Stir and serve, and thank Mamie.*

58. *Pissaladière*

This is a French Mediterranean version of a pizza, but a bit more elegant. Use brioche dough (see index), roll it ¼-inch thick, and spread on a baking sheet. Sprinkle with generous amounts of grated Parmesan and Swiss cheese, in equal quantities. Over this spread a layer of sliced onions that have been cooked until transparent in butter. Next comes tomato sauce, made by cooking peeled seeded chopped fresh tomatoes in olive oil until a paste, and seasoning with salt, pepper, and rosemary. Over this lay a symmetrical criss-cross pattern of anchovy fillets, and in the center of each square put a half a pitted ripe olive, cut side down. Bake in a 400° degree oven until the edges are nicely browned. Cut in squares to serve— hot, please.

GRASSHOPPER: *Shake well with ice: 1 ounce of green crème de menthe, 1 ounce of white crème de cacao, and 1 ounce of cream. Strain into a cocktail glass.*

59. *Lah Majoun*

This is a sort of Near East pizza, for which remark I hope I will be forgiven by Armenians, Syrians, and Italians. Prepare bread dough or a package of hot roll mix, and after the first rising, break off into balls the size of walnuts, and roll each one into a flat pancake. Arrange on greased cookie sheets and spread each one, clear to the edges, with filling. Bake at 425° for 20 minutes. The filling: Mix together 1 pound of ground beef or lamb, 1 cup of finely chopped onion, a large clove of garlic put through the press, 1 tablespoon of chopped mint, 1 cup of chopped parsley, some black pepper, 1½ teaspoons of salt, and 1 cup of tomato puree.*

*An ancient favorite, still good, is a stuffed olive wrapped in bacon and broiled. So is a tiny peanut butter sandwich, treated the same way.

60. *Cocktail Quiche*

Line a shallow 9-inch square baking dish with pastry and brush with slightly beaten egg white. Bake at 425° until the crust is set but not brown. Strew ½ pound of finely diced cooked ham over the bottom, and sprinkle over that 1½ cups of grated Swiss (from Switzerland, please) cheese. Combine 2 beaten eggs and 2 egg yolks with 1½ cups of scalded cream, ½ teaspoon of salt, a little freshly grated nutmeg, and a grinding or two of pepper. Pour this over the cheese and bake at 350° until the custard is set. Cut in 8 strips each way, and serve warm or, surprisingly, cold! Vary this by substituting crumbled cooked bacon, or shredded crab, lobster, or shrimp, or even chicken livers for the ham. All are superb!

BERMUDA HIGHBALL: *In a highball glass, with ice cubes, put 1½ ounces of dry gin, 1½ ounces of brandy, and 1 ounce of dry vermouth. Fill with ginger ale or charged water, garnish with lemon peel, and serve.*

61. *Tartes au Jambon*

Make tiny tart shells (see Index). Bake until lightly colored but not brown. Put a teaspoon of ground ham in each shell. Mix together 1 cup of hot cream, 3 eggs, slightly beaten, salt and pepper to taste, and a few gratings of nutmeg. Pour over the ham, sprinkle with a very little grated Parmesan, and bake in a 400° oven for 12 minutes, or until set.*

*Green Goddess dressing, a San Francisco specialty, is a particularly good dunk for shellfish or vegetables. Combine 6 chopped anchovies, 1 green onion, 2 tablespoons each of minced parsley and chives, 1 tablespoon of tarragon, 1½ cups of mayonnaise, and 2 tablespoons of lemon juice.

62. *Cheddar Pennies*

I have this recipe in my *West Coast Cook Book*, but I think it bears repeating. Combine ½ pound of well-aged dry Cheddar cheese with ¼ pound of butter, ½ teaspoon of salt, a dash of cayenne, and 1¼ cups of flour. Work all together with your hands, and chill. Roll about ¼-inch thick, cut in 1¼-inch rounds, arrange on cookie sheets, and chill again. Bake at 350° for 10 minutes, or until a pale pale gold.*

*Variations on this theme are legion. Before baking brush with slightly beaten egg, and sprinkle with chopped nuts or with sesame, poppy, caraway, or dill seeds. Or mix a little orégano or some chili powder in when you knead. Or, if you're the take-it-easy type, roll the dough in a cylinder like an icebox cookie, then chill, slice, and bake at once.

63. *Cheese & Onion Cookies*

Make the dough as for *Cheddar Pennies*, but work in 1 cup of finely minced green onions. Roll in marble-sized balls, put on ungreased cookie sheets, and chill. Bake at 350° for about 20 minutes, or until nicely browned. These may be served hot or cold, which means they can be made way ahead of time. What's more, they freeze like a dream.*

*Sandwich 2 slices of cucumber (not seedy ones) together with finely ground crab mixed with mayonnaise and chives, for an easy snack.

64. *Hot Anchovy Loaf*

One of the messiest appetizers I know, but one of the best for an outdoor party. Give each guest a fingertip towel wrung out in hot water and wrapped in foil—this for buttered fingers. Put a loaf of fresh homemade or good baker's bread in the freezer for a few hours to firm. Then trim off all crusts except the bottom one and, using a razor-sharp knife, slice the bread in thin thin slices right down to the bottom crust. Don't cut through that crust, though. Cream a pound of sweet butter and mix it with a whole 2-ounce tube of anchovy paste. Spread this mixture on each slice of bread, using the entire amount. Put on a cookie sheet and bake at 275° for an hour and a quarter, or until the edges have curled out and are crisply brown. Each guest tears off his own.

SIDECAR: *Shake well with ice: 2 ounces of Cognac, 1 ounce of Cointreau, and 1 ounce of lemon juice. Strain into a cocktail glass.*

65. *Fried Wun Tun*

This Chinese delicacy makes one of the best appetizers in the world, and its filling can be varied in umpty ways. If you are lucky, and live near a Chinese grocery store, you can buy the wun tun paste—squares of thin noodle dough all ready to fill and fry. But if you don't, take heart—the paste is easy to make. Mix together 3 cups of flour, 2½ teaspoons of salt, and 2 eggs. Knead until smooth and elastic, adding a little warm water if necessary. (If you have a KitchenAid with a dough hook, or a strong-armed and agreeable husband, there's nothing to it!) Form the dough in a ball, cover, and let stand for half an hour. Dust a pastry board with cornstarch and roll dough very thin. Cut into 3-inch squares. Take a hint from the Chinese, and stack them with a dusting of cornstarch between each; they won't stick. For fillings and cooking method, see next page.

FROZEN DAIQUIRI: *Place 2 cups of shaved ice in the blender. Add 4 ounces of light rum, a tablespoon of lime or lemon juice, and 2 teaspoons of powdered sugar. Blend to the consistency of snow and serve at once, with a straw.*

66. *Shrimp Wun Tun*

Make a filling by mixing 1 pound of ground raw shrimps, ¼ pound of raw lean pork, ¼ cup of minced green onions, ¼ cup of minced water chestnuts, 1 tablespoon of soy sauce, 1 tablespoon of Cognac or whiskey, and 1 tablespoon of cornstarch. When well blended, put a dab—about ½ teaspoonful —of the filling in the center of each wun tun square (see preceding page), fold in half diagonally, moisten just a little on either side of the filling, and again fold diagonally. Pinch firmly together and fry in deep fat at 370° until crisply bubbly brown. Drain and serve at once, or reheat in a moderate oven later.*

*The filled wun tun may stand several hours before frying, but in that case do not let them touch each other, and cover lightly to prevent drying out too much. Also, wun tun may be folded in many different ways, but they are much prettier and crisper if the edges are left free.

67. Other Wun Tun Fillings

Wun tun paste may be filled with almost anything, Chinese in character or not, and fried like the one on the preceding page.

Chicken-Ginger Filling: 1 pound of chopped raw chicken, ¼ cup of minced green onion, 1 tablespoon of grated ginger, 1 teaspoon of cornstarch, 1 tablespoon of sherry, 1 tablespoon of soy sauce. Mix well and use as for shrimp wun tun.

Filling of Brains: This filling is more like one for ravioli, but then some people call wun tun "Chinese ravioli." Simmer a pound of calves brains in 1 quart of water to which a teaspoon of salt and 2 tablespoons of vinegar have been added. Chill, clean, chop, and mix with ¼ cup of minced ham, ¼ cup of minced green onions, ½ cup of chopped pine nuts, ½ teaspoon of salt, 2 tablespoons of minced parsley, and a dash of pepper. Proceed as above.

BULLSHOT: *Over ice in an old-fashioned glass pour 2 ounces of vodka. Fill with chilled bouillon, and eat your cocktail or drink your dinner.*

68. *Tostados*

These are called various things in different parts of Mexico—*totopos*, for one. They are toasted tortillas, and are available in some parts of this country. If you can't get them, make them yourself by cutting tortillas—fresh or canned—into wedges, and frying in deep fat (380°) until crisp. If you can't even get tortillas, poor you, do ask your market to get you some tortilla flour, or *masa*, and make tortillas according to the directions on the bag. Roll the dough like pie crust and cut in circles, then bake on a slow griddle before deep frying as above. For uses of tostados, see next recipes. (NOTE: Tostados are also whole fried tortillas, garnished or not.)

BEER: *The more Mexican food you eat, the more you realize that beer is the drink to accompany it. Mexican beers are mostly of the Pilsner type, and mostly very good, although some of the larger breweries have managed to achieve mediocrity through over-production. Mexican beer, like our own, is highly carbonated, so should be well chilled.*

69. *Tostados With Beans*

Spread tostados with hot refried beans, then sprinkle with grated Cheddar or Jack cheese, and broil until the cheese melts. Canned refried beans are available, but homemade ones are better. Cook 1 pound of pink, red, or pinto beans until soft. Mash with their liquid, and season with salt to taste. Cook with 1 cup of lard or bacon fat until the beans are very soft and mushy, and richly crusty around the edges. Season with cumin or chili powder or garlic, if you want to, but the true Mexican beans just aren't.

TEQUILA: *This spicy Mexican liquor is a little strange to Northern palates, but you'll learn to love it. Sprinkle some salt in the hollow between thumb and forefinger, and hold a segment of lemon between those digits. Lick up the salt, drink a shot of Tequila, and suck the lemon, in rapid succession. Easy, swift, and* bueno.

70. *Tostados With Sardines*

This combination of flavors is very Mexican. Spread the tortillas with beans, as in the preceding recipe, put a piece of sardine on top, cross with a strip of canned green chile pepper, and heat in the oven for 3 or 4 minutes.

CRUSTA: *Rub the rim of a large wine glass with lemon, then spin in powdered sugar. Place in the glass a large twist of lemon or orange peel, and a cherry. Shake well with ice: a dash of bitters, 1 teaspoon each of lemon juice and maraschino, and 2 or 3 ounces of rum, gin, brandy, applejack, or whiskey. Strain into the prepared glass.*

71. *Tostados With Chorizo*

Chorizo is Mexican sausage, and if you can't find any, mix a tablespoon of chili powder with a pound of pork sausage meat. Cook, stirring, until brown and crumbly. Drain off fat and put a spoonful on each bean-spread tostado. Top with cheese or not, as desired, and serve hot. A good variation of this is to skip the beans and spread the tostado with guacamole, then top with the cooked chorizo. Don't heat these.

PLANTER'S PUNCH: *Shake vigorously with crushed ice: 3 ounces of Jamaica rum, 2 ounces of lemon juice, 1 ounce of sugar or simple syrup, and 2 or 3 dashes of bitters. Pour without straining into a tall glass. Pack glass to top with crushed ice, fill almost to top with charged water, and churn with a long spoon until glass starts to frost. Garnish with fruit, as desired, and serve with a straw.*

72. Elena's Chile Con Queso

Elena Zelayeta, author of "Elena's Secrets of Mexican Cooking," gave me this wonderful recipe. This should be served hot, from a chafing dish, but it isn't chili-hot unless you want it so. Cook a cup of minced onion in 2 tablespoons of butter until soft. Add a 28-ounce can of tomatoes and simmer until thick. Rinse seeds from a 4-ounce can of peeled green chiles, chop, and add. Make a cream sauce with 2 tablespoons each of butter and flour, and a cup of cream. When smooth and thick, combine with the tomato mixture. Season to taste with salt and, if you crave that extra heat, with a dash of Tabasco or chile Jalapeña. Two or three minutes before serving stir in ½ pound of finely diced Jack cheese—or Cheddar, if you can't get Jack. Stir until the cheese is partially melted, then allow your guests to dip in crisply fried tortillas, Fritos, cubes of bread, or meat balls impaled on sticks.

MEXICAN BOILERMAKER: *A straight shot of tequila washed down with a draught of cold beer. These can be pretty lethal, depending upon the number of rivets (shots) which go into each boiler (mug of beer).*

73. *Empanaditas*

These are little Mexican turnovers, very much like piroshki. Try making them with cream cheese pastry: 1 cup of flour, 1 small (3-ounce) package of cream cheese, ¼ pound (1 stick) of butter, and ¼ teaspoon of salt. Roll thin, cut in 2½-inch circles, and fill with any savory filling. Fold over, seal edges, and glaze or not, as you wish. Bake in a 375° oven for 15 minutes, or until brown.*

*FILLINGS: *Tuna fish mixed with anchovy paste is good; so is deviled ham, or grated cheese mixed with a little chopped green chile and mayonnaise; or chopped chili con carne (but sin frijoles!); or even well-seasoned corned beef hash.*

74. *Piroshki*

Like pasties and empanadas and turnovers, these are little tidbits with savory fillings. They may be made with pie crust, but they are also wonderful when roll dough is used; your own recipe or the packaged kind. Roll very thin after the first rising—about ⅛-inch. Cut it in small ovals (hah!) and put the filling in the middle, moisten the edges and bring *both sides* up to the top, pinching firmly together—they should look like little pointed dinner rolls when finished. Put them, sealed side *down*, on a well-buttered cookie sheet and glaze tops with an egg yolk slightly beaten with a little milk. Let rise 20 minutes, and bake at 400° until nicely browned. For fillings see next page.

THREE-MINUTE MILE: *Stir well with ice: 2 ounces of Cognac, 1 ounce of light rum, a dash of lemon juice, and a teaspoon of grenadine. Strain into cocktail glass.*

75. Fillings for Piroshki

(1) Chop 3 hard-boiled eggs and mix with an onion that has been chopped and sautéed in butter. Season with salt, pepper, and dill, and moisten with cream.

(2) Combine a cup of cooked salmon (canned is fine) with a small chopped sautéed onion, and moisten with sour cream. A chopped dill pickle may be added.

(3) Any cold cooked meat, or fish, or game, or fowl, chopped and mixed with gravy or cream sauce or sour cream, and seasoned with onion or any herb or spice. A fine way to use up leftovers!

MOSCOW MULE: *Squeeze into a highball glass ½ lime and drop in the rind. Add ice cubes and 2 or 3 ounces of vodka, and fill up with ginger beer. Stir and serve.*

76. Mushroom Turnovers

You'll need a large supply of these, as they go like mushroom turnovers. Pie pastry is again in order, rolled thin and cut into rounds or squares of about 2½ inches, I'd say. Fill and bake them like corned beef pasties. For the filling, clean and chop a pound of fresh mushrooms, stems and all, and cook slowly in 3 tablespoons of butter for about 10 minutes. Add 4 tablespoons of flour and 1½ cups of cream. Cook until thick and season with salt and pepper, and, if you wish, with sherry or tarragon or dill. Somehow I think anything detracts from the wonderful flavor of the mushrooms. Let cool before using.

HOT CIDER PUNCH: *Simmer a gallon of cider with a few sticks of cinnamon, ½ teaspoon of whole mace, and ½ teaspoon of whole allspice, for half an hour. Add 1 cup of Jamaica rum and 1 cup of brandy, and serve hot.*

77. Corned Beef Pasties

We first had these in a pub, in London, with a warm beer. They're even better with a cold cocktail. The English use a suet pastry, but your favorite pie crust does just as well. Roll it thin and cut in 3-inch circles. For the filling, sauté ½ cup of chopped onion in 2 tablespoons of butter. Add a pound of ground cooked corned beef (canned does nicely) and a chopped hard-boiled egg. Mix well, season with salt and pepper, and a little cream if it seems too stiff. Put a spoonful on each round of pastry and proceed as for empanaditas (see index), but bake at 375° for 18 minutes, or until brown.

JACK ROSE: *Shake well with ice: 2 ounces of applejack, ½ ounce of grenadine, and the juice of ½ lime. Strain into cocktail glass.*

78. Quesadillas Con Chile

You should make these little turnovers with *masa*, the ground corn that Mexicans use for tortillas, but that's hard to come by, so here is a North-of-the-Border version. Combine 1 large egg, ¾ cup of milk, 1½ cups of flour, 1½ cups of corn meal, 1½ teaspoons of salt, and 2 tablespoons of melted butter. Mix well, then roll thin and cut in 3-inch rounds. Put a piece of Jack cheese (about 2x½x¼ inches) and a piece of canned green chile on one half, fold over, and press firmly together. Bake in a 400° oven until nicely browned. If you omit the chile, you'll have just plain *quesadillas*.

MARGARITA: *Rub the rim of a cocktail glass with the rind of a lime, and spin in salt. Pour 2 ounces of tequila and ½ ounce of Cointreau over ice in a bar glass; add the juice of ½ lime, and stir. Strain into prepared glass.*

79. *Anchovy Cigarettes*

There are several ways to make these little thirstraisers. The easiest is to roll a fillet of anchovy in half a wun-tun square, seal with water, and fry in deep fat at 370° until brown. Another way is to fold anchovies in oblongs of plain or puff pastry, seal edges, brush with egg, and bake at 400° until richly amber. Still another way is to wrap the anchovies in thinly sliced buttered bread, and toast until brown.

MARTINI BOWL: *Jim Beard dreamed up this way of dealing with such active thirstraisers as those above. Place a block of ice in a punch bowl and make a gargantuan Martini therein. Serve in punch cups. The bowl is garnished with a lemon peel, cut in one continuous strip.*

80. *Blissfuls*

Amelia Bliss thought these up. Make cream cheese pastry as in empanaditas (see index), roll thin and cut in 2- or 2½-inch rounds. Spread with about ¼ teaspoon of anchovy paste, top with a pecan half, fold over, seal edges, and glaze tops with slightly beaten egg. Bake at 375° for 15 minutes, or until brown.

MARTINI: *Gin and dry (French) vermouth in your favorite proportions—from 2 to 1, to 10 to 1. Pour over ice in a bar glass or pitcher, stir gently (never shake) until well chilled, and strain into a cocktail glass. Add a green olive, a pickled onion, or a twist of lemon peel, and serve.*

81. *Tuna-Curry Puffs*

You'll want plain pastry for this. Roll it thin and cut in 2½- or 3-inch circles. Put a small spoonful of filling on half of each round, moisten edges with water and fold over, pressing well to seal. Fry in deep fat at 360° until puffy and brown. Drain and serve hot. These may be reheated after frying, or made up ahead of time and fried at the last minute. Filling: 1 can of grated tuna fish, 2 ounces of cream cheese (¼ of a half-pound cake, or ⅔ of a 3-ounce one), 2 teaspoons of curry powder, ¼ teaspoon of salt, ½ teaspoon of lemon juice, a very small clove of garlic put through a press or mashed with the salt, and a well-beaten egg. Mix thoroughly.

COWPUNCHER: *Shake well with shaved ice: 2 ounces of Bourbon and 1 ounce of cream. Strain into a cocktail glass.*

82. Orégano Cheese Olives

Combine ½ pound of grated sharp Cheddar, ¼ pound of butter, 1 cup of flour, ¼ teaspoon of salt, and ½ teaspoon of pulverized orégano. Mix well and form around well-drained pimiento-stuffed olives. Arrange on a cookie sheet, chill, and bake at 375° for 15 to 20 minutes, or until lightly colored.

DR. G'S GOLDEN REMEDY: *Stir well with ice: 2 ounces of dry gin, 1 ounce of Cointreau, and 1 ounce of orange juice. Strain into a cocktail glass and feel your health returning.*

83. *Ripe Olive Surprises*

Stuff large pitted ripe olives with a piece of green onion just large enough to fill the hole. Wrap in cream cheese pastry (see *empanaditas*, page . . . .) completely covering the olive. Bake in a 375° oven for 20 minutes, or until brown.

GLÖGG: *Heat 2 bottles of claret and 2 of port in a large kettle. In it place a cheesecloth bag containing 2 tablespoons of grated orange peel, 20 cardamom seeds, 5 or 6 cinnamon sticks, and 25 cloves. After 15 minutes of slow boiling, add 1 pound each of blanched almonds, and seedless raisins, and heat another 15 minutes. Remove kettle from fire, and bag from kettle. Place a pound of lump sugar on a wire grill over the kettle, and pour over a bottle of Cognac slowly. Light, and when sugar is melted, remove grill. Serve hot, with a few raisins and almonds in each mug . . . . öggh!*

84. *Canapé Maurigi*

When my friend, William Templeton Veach, sent me this recipe from Bonnétable, my first reaction was "so what?" That was before I tried them. He created them and named them for the Marquesa Esther Maurigi, who is famous for her cocktail parties in Florence. Cut the tops from firm red egg (or cherry) tomatoes and scoop out the insides. (Bill uses a tiny spoon for this, and I find a miniature French vegetable scoop ideal.) He also cuts off "the veriest end so it will stand up straight." This is tricky; it's easier, I think, to put the tomatoes in little bonbon cups of paper, or some contrived of aluminum foil. Drain the tomatoes, fill them with tomato aspic, allow to set, then put a rosette of mayonnaise on top of each one. The aspic I make with 1½ cups of tomato juice, a couple of slices each of onion and lemon, salt and pepper, and an herb bouquet of bay, basil, parsley, and thyme. Simmer; strain; add 1 envelope of plain gelatine in 2 tablespoons of water; correct seasoning, and cool until syrupy.*

* *Try rolling sharp creamy Cheddar into balls and sandwiching them between pecan halves; or wrapping them in an anchovy; or rolling in chopped ham, or green onion, or radish.*

85. Stuffed Cherry Tomatoes

The variations on this one are never-ending. Hollow out cherry or "egg" tomatoes, as in the preceding recipe. Here are some ways to fill them:

(1) Put half an anchovy, rolled, in the bottom; pipe in cream cheese on top; decorate with a sprinkle of parsley.

(2) Fill with deviled ham; put a slice of ripe olive on top.

(3) Fill with tuna fish mixed with a little mayonnaise and grated onion; put a feather of dill on top.

(4) Tuck a small stuffed olive inside.

(5) Stuff with Roquefort cheese, and top with a half pecan.

(6) Mix crisp bacon with Camembert cheese and fill tomatoes.

VITAMIN COCKTAIL: *Shake well with ice: 2 ounces of Jamaica rum, 1 ounce of grenadine, ½ ounce each of orange juice and lemon juice. Strain into a cocktail glass and throw away your pills.*

86. *Tomatoes Provençale*

These sound tricky and, frankly, they are. But worth it . . .
Using a very sharp knife, cut slices from the tops of cherry
tomatoes, press out the pulpy seeds, and remove core.
Although I sneer at the idea, I find that a small pair of pointed
scissors helps here. Turn upside down to drain. Make a filling
with the yolks of 2 hard-boiled eggs, 3 finely-minced
anchovies, a small pressed clove of garlic, ¼ cup of soft
butter and 1 tablespoon of minced parsley. Stuff tomatoes,
dip tops in minced parsley, spear on picks, and chill before
serving.

BLOODY MARY *(No. 1)*: *Pour over ice cubes in
a 6-ounce glass, 2 ounces of vodka. Fill with
tomato juice and squeeze in ¼ lemon. Add
salt and pepper, if you like, and a dash of
cayenne.*

87. Onions Escoffier

In France they serve *cornichons* with apéritifs; we think those pickles are as palate-numbing as the French believe our cocktails to be. Not *these* pickles, though, they are mild and crisp and delicious. Boil 2 quarts of small white pickling onions in water for 3 minutes. Pour off water and peel, scraping the root ends. Return to the kettle, cover with 2 bottles of white wine and 1 cup of white wine vinegar. Add ½ cup of olive oil, 3 tablespoons of tomato paste, ⅓ cup of sugar, a tablespoon of salt, a cup of white seedless raisins, and an herb bouquet of a couple of sprigs of thyme, a hot red chile pepper, and 2 bay leaves. Simmer slowly until the onions are tender and the sauce is thickened and golden. (If the onions are tender before the sauce is reduced, remove them and continue cooking the syrup.) Put in hot sterilized jars and seal.

BISHOP: *Fill a tumbler half full of cracked ice. Add a teaspoon of sugar and the juice of ½ lemon and ½ orange. Fill with claret or Burgundy, stir, and add 1 slice of orange and several dashes of rum.*

88. *Dilled Beans*

Calorie counters and epicures alike will bless you for these crisp flavorsome nibbles. Remove the ends from tender young green beans, but leave them whole. Blanch for 1 minute in boiling water, then pack in hot sterilized pint jars. To each jar add a small clove of garlic, crushed, a head of fresh dill or 2 teaspoons of Spice Islands dill weed, and a couple of chile pequins. Fill jars with a mixture of 2 cups each of boiling water and boiling vinegar, and ¼ cup of salt. Seal and hide for at least a month before you serve them, well chilled.

SHERRY: *Dry, or "cocktail," sherry should be served well chilled. Be sure it's a dry one rather than a dessert-type, such as the Amorosos and Olorosos, and the various "cream sherries." Dry sherry is generally lighter in color, and has a clean nutty flavor, quite unlike any other wine. Manzanilla and Amontillado are dry sherries, and "La Ina" is perhaps the dryest of all.*

89. *Pâté-Stuffed Mushrooms*

Select mushrooms of uniform size—1½ inches in diameter is good. Clean, remove stems, and sauté in a little butter for a minute. Add a few drops of water, cover, and cook slowly another 4 minutes. Cool and fill with pâté de foie gras (or with S.A.S. Pâté). Top with chopped pistachio nuts or with crisp crumbled bacon. Serve cool, but not chilled.

WINDWARD COOLER: *Fill a 10-ounce glass half full of crushed ice. Add 1 teaspoon of sugar, ½ lime (juice and peel), 10 fresh mint leaves, bruised, 2 ounces of light rum, and cold charged water to fill the glass. Stir to mix.*

90. *Stuffed Mushrooms*

Prepare mushroom caps as for mushrooms with pâté. Cool and stuff with a mixture of finely diced smoked turkey, finely diced celery, and a little mayonnaise. Sprinkle tops with minced parsley and serve cold, in little bonbon or foil cups. The fillings, of course, can be greatly varied. Ground ham and sour cream is a good one, so is chopped crisp bacon mixed with Camembert cheese. Or play your own tune.

SWEET MANHATTAN: *Stir well with ice: 2 ounces of rye or Bourbon, ½ ounce each of sweet vermouth and dry vermouth, and a dash of bitters. Strain into a cocktail glass, and add a maraschino cherry.*

91. *Stuffed Lichi Nuts*

This is an exotic recipe—one that tastes particularly good on a hot day. Drain canned lichi nuts and remove pits. Stuff cavities with a mixture of ½ pound of cream cheese, a pinch of salt, 1 tablespoon of Cognac, and either a tablespoon of grated ginger or 3 tablespoons of chopped toasted almonds. Serve chilled on picks.*

*Dried lichi nuts also make interesting appetizers. Remove their pits and stuff as above.

92. *Fruits With Prosciutto*

So this is an old idea! It all started in Italy, where either melon or fresh figs, served with paper-thin slices of prosciutto, is a favorite antipasto. We cut the fruits smaller and wrap them, fastening with the ubiquitous picks. But don't stop with these two fruits. Try cubes of pineapple, or pear, or papaya. Peaches are good, too, and so are avocados, though the latter needs a drizzle of lemon juice. Strawberries? Bananas? Mangoes? Why not?

VERMOUTH APÉRITIF: *Fill a cocktail glass two-thirds with cracked ice. Fill with Italian vermouth, and serve with a twist of lemon peel.*

93. *Artichokes With Shrimps*

Artichoke bottoms, if small, make a fine base for many savory bits: Shrimp salad, pâté, bacon and cheese, egg and anchovy salad, chicken livers, and such. Another nice way with artichokes is to serve the leaves with a little dab of mayonnaise at the eating ends, with a small shrimp nestled in it. And another is to tuck shrimps or other tasty tidbits into the middle of tiny hearts of artichokes, the kind that come canned. Or, if you have the tiny fresh ones in your market, cook and trim your own.

LOVING ELMORE: *A great restorative and surprisingly good to drink. Fill an 8-ounce glass half full of cold tomato juice, then fill up with cold beer. No stirring necessary, as the carbonation of the beer takes care of the mixing.*

94. *Stuffed Belgium Endive*

Stuffed celery you all know about, but perhaps stuffed Belgium endive is new to you. Just separate the head into leaves and pipe in the filling, if it is a smooth one, or spread it in with a knife if it isn't puréed. Some favored fillings: (1) Cream cheese softened with cream and mixed with anchovy paste or Roquefort cheese or deviled ham. (2) Cream cheese with red or black caviar, or chopped smoked oysters, or mashed sardines. (3) Pâté. (4) Any savory salad, such as lobster, crab, chicken, or duck.

PINK SPRING PUNCH:*Combine 1 bottle of Grenache Rosé, the zest (outside yellow skin) and juice of 1 lemon, 2 tablespoons of fine sugar, and 3 long strips of cucumber rind. Pour the punch over a block of ice in a punch bowl and add a bottle of pink Champagne.*

95. Caviar-Stuffed Celery

Red caviar, or salmon roe, can be used for this with pleasant results. Blend cream cheese with a little onion juice and salt. Select tender pieces of celery heart and half-fill (the long way) with red (or black) caviar. Using a pastry tube, pipe the cream cheese down the other side. Keep chilled until serving time.*

*And of course, there are the old favorites:
celery stuffed with Roquefort, or with pâté,
or with deviled ham, or . . . . . .

96. *Tidbits in Aspic*

Here is a type of appetizer that has innumerable possibilities, and one that is welcomed by weight-watchers. Its only drawback is the difficulty of serving. Some, such as shrimps and turkey cubes, can be impaled on toothpicks, but more fragile ones should be couched on a round of toast, or put in miniature tart shells or bonbon cases, or in the little foil cases I describe in the Introduction. As for the tidbits themselves, use any tasty morsel: a cube of chicken, a piece of lobster meat, or sweetbread or chicken liver. Or roll little balls of pâté de foie gras or any meat or fish paste, or cheese mixture. Chill them well, then dip into partially set, well-seasoned aspic, made stiffer than usual (1 tablespoon of plain gelatine to 1½ cups of liquid). The tidbits may be garnished after the first dipping has set, and again dipped. Miniature molds may be used, too, in which case unmold on a base of some kind.*

*Another good dipping aspic is made with 1 cup of mayonnaise, 1 tablespoon of lemon juice, 1 envelope of plain gelatine, and ¼ cup of water.

97. *Eggs Béarnaise*

Use leftover Béarnaise sauce for this, or make a batch the quick way, in a Waring Blendor. (Cook 3 chopped shallots and ¼ teaspoon of tarragon in ¼ cup of tarragon vinegar until the vinegar is absorbed. Add a pinch of dry mustard and ½ cup (¼ pound) of butter; heat until the butter is bubbly. Put 3 egg yolks in the blendor and turn on high for 30 seconds. Add the hot butter mixture gradually with the blendor turned on low [or add a spoonful at a time, turning on high for a few seconds between each addition]. As the mixture thickens, the butter can be added faster.) Mash the yolks of hard-boiled eggs smooth and add Béarnaise to moisten. Correct seasoning, adding additional salt. Fill egg whites and tuck a little cube of ham (Bayonne would be perfect) in the top of each egg.

CALIFORNIA SUNSHINE: *We were introduced to this pleasant apéritif by M. Louis Vaudable, at Maxim's, in Paris. In a large wine glass put ½ cup of cold orange juice, and fill to the top with iced Champagne. Little did we know it was named for home!*

98. *Eggs Breton*

Make Béarnaise as in the recipe for Eggs Béarnaise (see preceding recipe). Mash a large can of drained sardines, mix with the yolks of a dozen hard-boiled eggs, and add Béarnaise to moisten. Heap high in the egg whites, and garnish each with a tiny section of a lemon slice, peel removed.

ROB ROY: *Stir well with ice: 2 ounces of Scotch whisky, 1 ounce of sweet (Italian) vermouth, and 2 dashes of bitters. Strain into a cocktail glass, and serve with a twist of lemon peel.*

99. *Eggs Niçoise*

Remove the yolks from a dozen hard-boiled eggs. Mash half of them with 4 finely minced anchovies, a tablespoon of chopped capers, a teaspoon of mustard, a tablespoon of finely minced ripe olives, a teaspoon of olive oil, and a teaspoon of Cognac. Divide among the halved egg whites. Mash the remaining yolks smooth, mix with mayonnaise, and pipe around the edges of the filling, using a pastry tube.

FRENCH '75: *In a highball glass put ½ ounce of lemon juice, sugar to taste, and 2 ounces of dry gin. Add plenty of ice cubes, fill to the top with chilled Champagne, and stir.*

100. *Eggs Annecy*

Hard-boil a dozen eggs and shell. Remove yolks and mash well. Mix with ¼ cup of finely minced onion and ½ cup of finely minced mushrooms that have been cooked in 3 tablespoons of butter. Season with salt, a little freshly ground nutmeg, and enough mayonnaise to bind, and fill whites with the mixture.

SHERRY COBBLER: *Fill a tumbler ⅔ full of cracked ice. Add ½ teaspoon of sugar and a teaspoon of orange juice. Fill with sherry, stir slightly, decorate with fruit, and serve.*

101. *Eggs Nantua*

The classic recipe calls for crayfish, but shrimps will do nicely. Hard-boil the eggs, shell, and scoop out the yolks. Cut cooked crayfish, shrimps, or crab meat in tiny dice, and mix with seasoned mayonnaise. Heap the whites with this mixture. Dissolve a teaspoon of plain gelatine in a tablespoon of water; melt over hot water, and mix with ½ cup of mayonnaise. Smooth over the top of each egg, and garnish with a cut-out piece of truffle (the classic way), or with a slice of ripe olive. Allow to set in the refrigerator before serving. Well, what would *you* do with the egg yolks?

GIN *or* VODKA & TONIC: *Just add quinine tonic to 2 or 3 ounces of gin or vodka, and ice, in a highball glass. Squeeze in half a lime, peel and all, and stir gently.*

102. *Eggs Carème*

These are not to be confused with the hot dish, made with artichoke hearts and Nantua sauce. Hard-boil 6 eggs, crack shells under cold water, and leave soaking until cool. Remove shells, cut in halves, and remove yolks. Cut tiny slices from bottoms of whites so that they will stand upright. Sauté 3 chopped shallots in 3 tablespoons of butter until wilted. Add ¼ cup of finely chopped sorrel leaves. Mix with well-mashed egg yolks, season with necessary salt and pepper, and a few drops of cream or lemon juice. Fill whites with this mixture and sprinkle with minced parsley.

TORPEDO: *Stir well with ice: 2 ounces of apple-jack, 1 ounce of brandy, and a dash of gin. Strain into a cocktail glass, and damn the torpedoes!*

103. Deviled Eggs, Indienne

Here I go with deviled eggs again, but they are always a favorite. Hard-boil a dozen of them, peel, halve, and cut a little slice from the bottom of each so they will stand up straight. Mash the yolks and mix them with 2 teaspoons of lemon juice, 2 teaspoons of curry powder, a teaspoon of soy sauce, and enough mayonnaise to make soft but not soupy. Add salt to taste and, using a pastry tube, pipe into the egg whites, leaving a little hollow in the center. In said hollow put about ½ teaspoon of Major Grey or other good chutney, chopped.

JUBILEE FIZZ: *Shake well with ice: 2 ounces of dry gin and 2 ounces of unsweetened pineapple juice. Strain into highball glass and fill with chilled Champagne.*

104. *Cucumber Cups*

Nice for a hot day—and for dieters, too! Select slender cucumbers and peel with a garnishing knife—the kind that cuts grooves or scallops. Slice off ends and cut cucumbers in ¾-inch slices. Scoop out insides, leaving a bottom. A small French ball cutter does this beautifully. Sprinkle with salt and turn upside-down to drain. Fill with almost any kind of fish salad: salmon, lobster, or sardine (especially sardine). Or fill with finely minced celery and green onion mixed with a little sour cream or mayonnaise, or for dieters, yoghurt.*

*An especially good filling is cream cheese seasoned with salt, chives, and minced dill.

105. *Rouge et Noir*

So simple this. Crisp red radishes, well scrubbed and with a bit of their green leaves remaining, are couched on a bed of ice along with huge black olives. On small inside leaves of romaine arrange whole boneless sardines, and let them share the icy bed. Lemon wedges and curls of sweet butter complete this pretty picture, and a napkin-covered basket of tiny hot rolls or baking powder biscuits are nearby. You'll want to serve little plates and spreaders with this appetizer.

SAZERAC: *In a well-chilled old-fashioned glass put a few drops of Pernod, and roll it around to coat the inside thoroughly. In a mixing glass, stir well with ice: 2 ounces of Bourbon, 2 dashes of bitters, and a dash of Italian vermouth. When good and cold, strain into the prepared glass and garnish with a twist of lemon.*

106. *Les Creditées*

These are simply raw vegetables, served with or without a sauce for dunking. In France they use halves or quarters of tiny artichokes and raw asparagus, as well as all the more usual celery, celeriac, green pepper strips, green onions, radishes, carrot and turnip sticks, cauliflower buds, cucumber sticks, crisp watercress, cherry tomatoes, endive, and zucchini. For a sauce, try mixing a pint of sour cream with 1/4 cup of Dijon mustard, a tablespoon of tarragon vinegar, 1/4 cup each of capers and chives and parsley. Or use a pint of sour cream with 1 can of minced ripe olives, a crushed clove of garlic, 2 teaspoons of chopped dill, and a tablespoon of lemon juice. Or just use mayonnaise, a good one made with olive oil and lemon juice.*

*Aioli *makes a wonderful sauce, too. See the index for the recipe.*

107. *Basic Dip*

Combine ½ pound of cream cheese and ½ cup of sour cream. To this add any chopped fish, such as smoked oysters, crab, clams, or sardines; any chopped meat, such as ham or chicken livers; any herb, such as chives or tarragon; spice, such as chili or curry powder; and such things as caviar, capers, and onions. No dried onion soup, please! Don't forget salt.

INTERPLANETARY: *Shake well with ice: 2 ounces of rum, 2 ounces of gin, 2 ounces of Bourbon, and 2 ounces of port wine. Strain into two cocktail glasses, and watch the stars go by.*

108. *Aioli*

A lusty gusty dip that should be served only to garlic lovers. Try it with crisp raw vegetables: celery, carrot sticks, raw asparagus, cucumber sticks (seeds discarded), and little cherry tomatoes. Crush 5 or 6 peeled garlic cloves in ¾ teaspoon of salt until liquid. Add 2 egg yolks and beat well, then, a drop at a time at first, beat in ½ cup of olive oil. It will thicken like mayonnaise. Further season with some freshly ground black pepper and a few drops of lemon juice.

BLUE MONDAY: *Stir well with ice: 3 ounces of vodka, 1 ounce of Cointreau, and a dash of blue vegetable coloring. Strain into cocktail. (If you're allergic to blue drinks, leave out the coloring.)*

109. *Brandade de Morue*

This is a hot dip that is rich and garlicky. It is especially good with crisp bread sticks or with chilled—and also crisp—celery. Cover a pound of salt codfish with water and bring to a boil. Pour off salt water, add more, and cook for 10 minutes, or until tender. Drain, remove bones, and grind 2 or 3 times, using a fine blade. Put in the top of a double boiler, over hot water. Heat together ½ cup each of butter (¼ pound) and olive oil. Add to the fish, a little at a time, stirring constantly until smooth and hot. Add a goodly amount of freshly ground black pepper and 2 cloves of garlic that have been put through a press or pounded in a mortar.

MILK PUNCH: *Over ice cubes in a highball glass pour 2 ounces each of Jamaica rum and Cognac. Fill to the top with ice-cold milk, and grate a little nutmeg over the top.*

110. *Canapé Suédois*

You'll want a good Swedish-type rye bread for this, and thinly sliced smoked salmon, preferably some that hasn't been packed in oil. Mix a tablespoon of grated horseradish with ¼ pound of butter, spread the bread with this, lay on a slice of the smoked salmon, and garnish with ½ slice of paper-thin lemon, twisted into a curl.

GLOW WINE: *A hot drink on a cold grey day is sometimes just right. Pour 2 bottles of dry red wine into a heavy saucepan; add ¼ cup of granulated sugar, 6 cloves, and the thinly pared peel of half a lemon. Bring to a boil and serve quickly in glasses with a slice of orange.*

111. *Herring Canapés*

Bone and chop smoked herring, and mix 1 cup of it with ¾ cup of cream sauce. Heap on toast, sprinkle with grated Parmesan, and broil until brown. Herring tidbits, or kippered herring in cans, may be used in this recipe.

RUM SCAFFA: *Place in a cocktail glass a dash of bitters, and 1 ½ ounces each of Benedictine and rum. Stir and serve. Scaffas are always served unchilled and undiluted.*

112. *Green Onion Rolls*

Slice very fresh white bread very thin and remove crusts. It's easier to slice if you first put it in the freezer for a few hours. Spread each slice with soft butter. Trim tender green onions a little longer than the bread slices, put on bread, and roll tightly. Pack cut side down and close together, and chill until serving time. These can be varied by trimming onions the same size as the bread, and dipping ends in mayonnaise and then in minced parsley at one end, paprika at the other.

PHILIP'S PUNCH: *Mix together 4 bottles of dry white table wine, 1 bottle (4/5 quart) each of Cognac and gold label rum, and ½ can of frozen concentrated lemonade. Add 2 quarts of charged water, and pour over a large block of ice in a punch bowl. The quantities of rum and Cognac may be cut in half without changing the flavor.*

113. *Celery-Anchovy Rolls*

Simple as these are, they are among my favorites. Slice bread as for green onion rolls (see index), spread with softened sweet butter. Lay strips of anchovy fillets inside tender pieces of celery hearts, cut to the length of the bread. Roll bread around celery and pack close together. Keep chilled until serving time.

UNCLE HARRY'S PUNCH: *Over a block of ice in a punch bowl pour 2 bottles of Rhine wine, 1½ cups of orange juice, 1½ cups of lemon juice, 6 ounces of Curaçao, 6 ounces of gold label rum, 2 bottles of charged water, and 2 bottles of Champagne. Garnish with mint leaves and fresh fruit.*

114. *Onion Brioche*

James Beard, America's foremost gastronomist, introduced me to this delight. It's his favorite, and I don't wonder! Slice brioches, or a brioche loaf, ¼-inch thick, and cut in circles. Spread with well-seasoned mayonnaise, and sandwich two together with a thin slice of onion between. Roll the edges in mayonnaise and then in very finely minced parsley. Keep chilled until serving time. These can be made with bread but they are not as spectacular. For a quick brioche, try this: Soften a cake of yeast in ¼ cup of warm water. Add 1 table-spoon of sugar and ¾ teaspoon of salt, and 1 cup of flour. Let stand until doubled in bulk, then beat in 1½ bars (¾ cup) of soft but not melted butter, 3 eggs, 3 egg yolks, and 3 more cups of flour. Again let rise, then put in well-greased cylin-drical bread pans (the kind that hinge in the middle), or in ordinary loaf pans, and let rise again until double. Bake at 400° for 25 to 40 minutes—the time depending on the pan. Makes 3 cylinders or 2 loaves.

SPRITZER: *Put 4 ounces of white wine in a highball glass with ice cubes. Fill with charged water.*

115. S. A. S. Snitters

Scandinavian Airlines System, famous for its open-faced sandwiches, called smörrebrod, also serves a snack called a snitter, which is a miniature smörrebrod. There's nothing better for an appetizer. Here are a few of their most popular ones: (1) Paper-thin slices of rare roast beef laid on buttered bread in ruffles, and garnished with fried onions, a pickled onion, and a small slice of dill pickle. (2) Buttered rye bread with sliced S.A.S. liver pâté (see index), garnished with thinly sliced cucumber and a sprig of dill. (3) Buttered bread with smoked salmon, garnished with a strip of cold scrambled egg and dill. (4) Rye bread spread with pork drippings, with sliced pork and a garnish of chopped aspic. (5) Buttered bread with pickled herring, garnished with pimiento and chopped raw onion. (6) Buttered bread with any cheese, and garnished with lettuce or cress, and pimiento and olives.*

*These snitters may be a full-sized sandwich cut in quarters, or the "snitter de luxe" made on small rounds or squares of bread.

116. *Petits Choux*

Choux, or cream puff paste, is the basis of many excellent appetizers. Cook ¼ pound of butter with 1 cup of milk until the butter is melted. Dump in, all at once, 1 cup of flour and ¼ teaspoon of salt. Stir over the heat until it forms a big mass in the middle of the pan—this happens almost at once. Cool slightly, then beat in 4 whole eggs, one at a time. Drop by teaspoonfuls or, even better, from a pastry bag in marbles, on cookie sheets, and bake at 375° for 30 minutes, or until no moisture shows on top. If not cooked long enough, they will collapse, if cooked too much they will become brittle and break while being filled. In other words, watch it! When cool, slit each puff near the bottom, press open and fill. If that is too difficult, cut off top, fill, and replace top.*

*For fillings for petits choux, use pâté, deviled ham, cheese, any fish or meat paste, or lobster, crab, chicken, or shrimp salad.

117. *Tiny Tart Shells*

These can be filled with any number of delectable things, many of them made from little dabs of this and that. The shells freeze beautifully, so make yourself a batch when you have a minute to spare. For the pans use the little doll's muffin tins that can be found in most toy departments. Snip and bend them out of their frames, using tin snips and pliers, or make pans using triple layers of heavy aluminum foil. Make pastry —I use 2 cups of flour, ⅓ cup each of butter and lard, 1 teaspoon of salt, and water to just hold together. Roll thin, cut in circles, and press over the bottoms of the pans, pinching off the surplus at the edges. Put on a cookie sheet, pastry side up, and bake in a 425° oven for 5 minutes. Now place another cookie sheet on top to keep the bottoms flat, reduce heat to 350°, and bake until lightly browned. Let cool before removing from the pans. See the next page for suggested fillings.

WHITE WINE COCKTAIL: *Put a dash of bitters in a cocktail glass, then fill with very cold Rhine wine—a Riesling or Johannisberger is good. Add a small twist of lemon peel and serve.*

118. *Cold Fillings for Tiny Tarts*

You can really play your own tune when it comes to filling these little tart shells (see preceding page). Here are a few hints:

(1) Finely minced lobster meat, mixed with mayonnaise, topped with chopped dill.

(2) Chopped chicken salad, topped with chopped toasted almonds.

(3) Mashed avocado, seasoned with mayonnaise and grated onion.

(4) Chopped ham mixed with sour cream.

(5) Chopped shrimps and mayonnaise, seasoned with curry or tarragon.

SHERRY OLD-FASHIONED: *Moisten ½ teaspoon of sugar with a dash or two of bitters. Add ice cubes and 3 or 4 ounces of dry sherry, and stir. Add a good twist of lemon peel and serve. May be garnished with cherry, orange, and such, if you like fruit salad drinks.*

119. *Hot Fillings for Tiny Tarts*

Like the cold fillings, anything goes in these little shells. Here are a few to start you on your way:

(1) Creamed finnan haddie with a little chopped green pepper.

(2) Chopped sautéed kidneys, with Cognac and a little cream.

(3) Creamed shrimps with dill.

(4) Curried chicken, or crab, or ...

(5) Mushrooms in cream, or ditto sweetbreads.

(6) Turkey in Mornay sauce, or just plain Mornay sauce.

JAVA LIBRE: *Put several ice cubes in a high-ball glass. Pour over 2 or 3 ounces of Jamaica rum, and fill with cold black coffee. You can add cream and sugar, if you like, but remember Jamaica rum is made from molasses.*

120. *Hors d'Oeuvre à la Russe*

A spectacular, this. Fill a large silver tray with finely crushed ice, and in it sink 3 glass or silver bowls. Fill one with caviar, one with mayonnaise, and one with Russian dressing. In the remaining spaces on the ice arrange nests of tender leaves of Boston lettuce. In these have various seafoods: chunks of boiled lobster, tender pink shrimps, cracked Dungeness crab or king crab legs; around the entire edge have oysters and/or clams on the half shell. Garnish with generous wedges of lemon, big plump ripe olives, and crisp tender rosy radishes. Enough said.

VOLGA BOATMAN: *Stir well with ice: 2 ounces of vodka, 2 ounces of Cognac, and 2 ounces of orange juice. Strain into cocktail glass.*

121. *Oysters With Caviar*

The most difficult thing about this appetizer is paying for it. Arrange small oysters on the half shell on a tray filled with finely crushed ice. Put a teaspoonful (oh, a half-teaspoonful, if you want!) of caviar on each oyster, and have plenty of lemon wedges here and there between the oysters.

CHABLIS: *The best possible drink with oysters is a fine chilled Chablis, dry and hard, but with lovely overtones of fruitiness. This affinity seems to be of the earth itself, for the hillside vineyards surround the town of Chablis like a great oyster shell.*

122. Smoked Salmon Rolls

Mix a 4-ounce can of minced ripe olives and a tablespoon of minced dill with ½ pound of cream cheese, softened with a few drops of cream. Spread generously on thinly-sliced smoked salmon, roll, and cut in 1-inch pieces with scissors. Serve on picks.*

*A variation of this is to spread bread with the cheese mixture, top with a slice of the salmon, and cut in squares for serving.

123. *Seviche*

This is a raw fish appetizer from Acapulco, where they usually use corbina or pompano, but any firm-fleshed fish will do. Remove skin and bones from 2 pounds of it and dice. Put in a porcelain or glass dish and cover with 2 cups of lemon or lime juice, and let stand in the refrigerator for 3 or 4 hours. Drain, add 2 chopped onions, 1 can of green chiles, chopped, 2 tomatoes, peeled, seeded, and chopped, 2 teaspoons of salt, and a little oregano and pepper. Serve in little shells with tostados (fried tortillas) or Fritos as an accompaniment.

BACARDI SPECIAL: *Shake well with ice: 2 ounces of light rum, 1 ounce of dry gin, the juice of ½ lime, and a teaspoon of grenadine. Strain into cocktail glass.*

124. *Smoked Fish Assortment*

This isn't a recipe, it's just a thought. Have a large tray arranged with an appetizing assortment of smoked and/or kippered fish—salmon, whitefish, butterfish, eels, sardines, Alaska cod, herring, and whatever your area affords. Have parsley and lemon as a garnish, and another tray of buttered sliced bread. Good bread, please, like Jewish or Danish rye, pumpernickel, and a good French or Italian loaf.

ZENITH: *In a highball glass, over ice cubes, pour 1 tablespoon of pineapple juice and 3 ounces of dry gin. Fill with charged water and serve with a pineapple stick.*

125. *Smoked Whitefish Platter*

This is one of those simple, but very effective appetizers. Bed a whole smoked whitefish on a long, parsley-covered platter. Pull back the skin from the top side and cut off at the backbone. Surround with big wedges of lemon. Have plenty of thinly-sliced buttered rye or pumpernickel bread on hand. The fish lifts easily from the bone, so the guests may help themselves. Small plates and forks are a nice touch, though not necessary, as the fish can be put on the bread and eaten out of hand.

BAMBOO COCKTAIL: *Half dry sherry, half vermouth (sweet or dry, depending on your palate); add a dash of Angostura and orange bitters, and pour over ice. Don't shake.*

126. *Caviar*

You don't have to be a gastronomical snob to vote this the best of all possible appetizers. It doesn't take imagination but it *does* take money, for there's no use serving it unless you have the *best* and plenty of it. For me there is only one way to serve it—in a bowl, nested in ice, and accompanied by hot crisp buttered toast. Lemon wedges should be at hand, also finely chopped onion and hard-boiled egg, for those who want it, though a true caviar connoisseur will eschew such trimmings. Red caviar, to my mind, is better than a poor grade of sturgeon roe, though I prefer to call it salmon roe, which it is.

CHAMPAGNE: *As long as we're going all out with the caviar, we might as well have the most festive of wines with it. The Champagne should be a brut, as the sweeter ones will not go so well with the saltiness of the caviar. It should be well chilled and served in tulip glasses or goblets. It's fun to pop the cork, but a lot of those precious bubbles go with it, so it's wiser to pull it gently. Have plenty, for even the most temperate will want a refill or two.*

127. *Marinated Herring*

Herring addicts, and there are many, think this is the best of all possible appetizers. Certainly it's the easiest, if you purchase the herring fillets, or tidbits, already marinated. Serve them in a dish garnished with thinly sliced raw onion and, for color, some strips of pimiento. Have buttered dark bread on hand, and plenty of sour cream. Here, again little plates are a great help, though if the pieces of bread and fish are small enough they could be popped whole into the mouth —a Scandinavian version of *bonne bouche?*

HIGHLAND FLING: *Shake well with ice: 2 ounces of Scotch whisky, 1 teaspoon of sugar, and 4 ounces of milk. Strain into an old-fashioned glass, sprinkle with nutmeg, and serve.*

128. *Charcuterie*

Although this term includes galantines and pâtés and other elaborate meat dishes made of pork, I'd stick to the various pork sausages and cold cuts that can be purchased ready to eat. But do see that they are the very finest, for inferior sausages and so-called "luncheon meats," made with cereal fillers, can be an abomination. So go to the best delicatessen or sausage shop you know, and get an assortment: mortadella, Thuringer, metwurst, Bologna, Braunschweiger, cervelat, head cheese, blood sausage, salami—any or all. They don't all *have* to be pork. Have sliced Virginia or Italian ham, too, if you want, but cut the slices in small pieces. Arrange prettily on a large platter. Have sliced and buttered breads present, too—good ones, like pumpernickel, and Russian and Swedish rye—and two or three kinds of prepared mustard.

GIN & BITTERS: *In great-grandmother's day, this was known as the "whore's drink" and perhaps it was. It's worthy of more respectability, however. Pour 2 or 3 ounces of gin over ice in an old-fashioned glass. Add 4 to 6 dashes of bitters. The flavor is no less lovely than the pretty pink color.*

129. *Turkey Tidbits*

If dark meat is your favorite, you'll welcome this way to use the breast that goes begging. Or purchase the white meat from a dealer who sells turkey parts, and cook it. Cut the meat in neat uniform ¾-inch cubes. Dip each into mayonnaise that has been well seasoned with curry, chili powder, or tarragon, then roll in finely chopped salted almonds. Easy as that!*

*A hot version of this is to dip the turkey cubes in a mixture of melted butter and sherry, with a little soy sauce, then roll them in toasted sesame seeds.

130. *Chipped Beef Pillows*

Have chipped beef sliced a little thicker than usual so that it won't tear. Mix ½ pound of cream cheese with either 2 tablespoons of grated onion or grated horseradish. Add enough cream to make it pliable. Form the cheese into sausages the length of the slices of beef, and place on one side. Roll the beef around it and "paste" the edges with a little of the cheese. Cut into ¾-inch pieces with a pair of scissors (this makes them "pillow" shape), and garnish the top of each with a rosette of cream cheese.

SHERRY FLIP: *Shake well with cracked ice: 4 ounces of sherry, 1 egg, and 1 teaspoon (or less) of powdered sugar. Strain into glass, and sprinkle nutmeg on top.*

131. *Roquefort-Cognac Crisps*

The crisp part is apple—½-inch slices of cored but unpeeled red ones. Dip them quickly in lemon juice so that they won't darken, and spread with a mixture of ½ pound of Roquefort cheese blended with ¼ cup of butter or cream cheese, and a tablespoon of Cognac. Simple and good.

FRUIT PUNCH *(for 50) (Non-alcoholic): Boil 2 cups of sugar in 1 cup of water for 5 minutes; add a cup of strong hot tea, 1 cup of grenadine, 1 cup of lemon juice, 2 cups of pineapple juice, and let stand for 30 minutes. Add 4 quarts of ice water, 2 cups of cleaned halved strawberries, and a quart of charged water. Pour over ice in a punch bowl.*

132. *Mammoth Cheese Balls*

These are just large balls of various spreads, rolled in some colorful tidbit, and meant for guest service. Do have more than one—all three if the party is large.

Mexican: Combine 2 pounds of soft grated Cheddar cheese, 1 can of minced ripe olives, and 2 cans of chopped peeled green chiles. Cream well, form in a large ball, and chill. Roll completely in minced parsley.

Oriental: Two pounds of cream cheese, 2 cups of drained crushed pineapple, 2 tablespoons of curry powder, 2 tablespoons of soy sauce, ¼ cup of grated candied ginger. Roll in chopped salted almonds.

French: One pound of Roquefort cheese, ½ pound of butter, ½ pound of hoop cheese, 2 jiggers of Cognac. Roll in minced herbs: parsley, chives, and tarragon.*

Small balls, impaled on picks, can be made with the very same mixtures, and rolled in the same coatings.

133. *Camembert Balls*

This recipe is from my *Holiday Cook Book*. It is, I said there, divinely simple. Select a whole ripe Camembert, put it in a bowl just large enough to hold it, and completely cover with white wine. Let stand overnight, scrape off discolored outside, and mash cheese very smooth. Combine with ¼ pound of butter, chill, roll in balls the size of butter balls, and then in chopped salted almonds. Serve cold with *hot* toasted crackers.

WHISKEY SOUR: *Shake well with ice: 2 or 3 ounces of any whiskey, the juice of ½ lemon, and ½ teaspoon of sugar. Pour into sour glass, ice and all, and garnish with fruit, if desired. The proportion of lemon juice and sugar may be altered to suit individual tastes.*

134. *Kippered Cheese*

. . . and I don't mean skippered! Canned kippers, inexpensive and good, can be mashed with equal parts of cream cheese, seasoned with lemon juice, scraped onion, and a dash of cayenne. Roll in balls, then in finely minced parsley or chives. Chill and serve on toothpicks, or on rounds of toast.

CARIOCA: *Moisten the rim of a cocktail glass with a piece of lime peel, then spin in fine granulated sugar. Shake well with ice: the juice of ½ lime, ½ teaspoon of sugar, and 2 ounces of gold label rum. Strain into the prepared glass.*

135. *Roquefort Roll*

This is a slice-it-yourself appetizer, not as messy as a dip and a great deal tastier than many. That's because it is made of the world's most famous cheese. Mash a pound of Roquefort cheese with ¼ pound of butter, ½ pound of cream cheese, a jigger of Cognac, and 2 tablespoons of finely minced chives. When well blended, form into a cylinder about 1½ inches in diameter, roll until completely covered in chopped toasted almonds, and chill. Put on a board surrounded with rounds of Melba toast or crackers, or—and this is for me—slices of French rolls, and provide a knife.

WARD EIGHT: *Shake well with ice: 4 ounces of rye or Bourbon, 1 ounce each of lemon and orange juice, and a teaspoon of grenadine. Strain into a sour or old-fashioned glass and fill up with charged water. Garnish with a cherry and an orange slice.*

136. *Date With a Cheddar*

A cinch, these. Cut pieces of well-aged Cheddar cheese in oblong pieces, a bit longer than a date pit. Soak them for a few hours in Cognac to cover. Remove pits from dates, substitute marinated cheese—voila! These can be wrapped in bacon and broiled, but I can't see much advantage unless you really *like* to work.

PEACH BOWL: *Peel 6 large, very ripe peaches and slice them in eighths. Put the slices in a punch bowl and sprinkle them with ¼ cup of fine sugar and ½ cup of Cognac. Let the fruit stand several hours, then pour over it 3 bottles of iced Champagne. Serve with a slice of peach in each glass.*

137. *Cannibal Balls*

Aficionados of *boeuf tartare* will go for these in a big way, for raw beef is what they are. Have a pound of fine sirloin or tenderloin ground fine. Mix it with 1½ teaspoons of salt, a small onion, grated, a dash of cayenne, and ½ teaspoon of freshly ground black pepper. Mix thoroughly with your hands and form in marble-sized balls. Dip in slightly beaten egg, then roll thoroughly in finely minced parsley. Chill and serve on toothpicks. These may be varied by wrapping an anchovy fillet around each ball, or by rolling in chives, or a mixture of parsley, chives and marjoram. Salubrious, and said to be sobering!*

*If you are of the spread-your-own school, don't make the balls, just mound the seasoned beef and sprinkle with parsley. Your guests can take it from there.

138. *Rillettes de Tours*

This hearty French peasant dish is very right at an informal party—particularly one served al fresco. Chop a pound of rather fat fresh pork, preferably from the shoulder, in small pieces—not larger than a pea. Put them in a heavy pan with a small sliced onion, an herb bouquet consisting of 3 sprigs of parsley, a sprig each of rosemary and thyme, and a bay leaf. Add a cup of water and simmer until the water is absorbed, pressing the pork with a spoon occasionally to express the fat. Add another cup of water, again cook down, and repeat a third time, each time pressing. Let cubes brown the last time, then pour off fat, pressing it all out; reserve. Add a teaspoon of salt to the meat and pack in a little crock. Heat the fat, pour it over the pork, cover, and keep refrigerated until used. If you have no cover for your crock, you might try the classic French method of covering with paper that has been dipped in Cognac.

DRY MANHATTAN: *Stir gently with ice: 3 or 4 ounces of rye or Bourbon whiskey, 1 ounce of dry vermouth and a dash of bitters. Strain into a cocktail glass and add a twist of lemon peel or a cherry.*

139. *Chicken Liver Pâté*

There's nothing new about chicken liver pâté except the additions that you make on your own. Cook a pound of chicken livers in 1/4 cup of butter for 10 minutes. Chop, coarsely or fine according to your preference, and blend with 1/2 cup of chopped onion that has been cooked with a cup of chicken fat, 2 teaspoons of salt, a dash of cayenne, a jigger of Cognac, and whatever seasoning suits your fancy. Some suggestions: freshly grated nutmeg and/or ground cloves; tarragon; ginger—either powdered or green-grated; bits of crisp bacon; chopped nuts; truffles; ripe olives. Pack the mixture in little pots and keep chilled until serving time. And try accompanying it with slices of fresh crusty bread instead of crackers.

CHAMPAGNE COOLER: *Half-fill a tall glass with cracked ice. Pour in 2 ounces of Cognac and 2 ounces of Cointreau; stir, and fill with cold Champagne.*

140. S.A.S. Liver Pâté

I first had this pâté when flying "over the pole" from Los Angeles to Copenhagen. Even when served in the same company with those superlative S.A.S. meals, this was outstanding. Later Viggo Hansen, head chef of the Scandinavian Airlines System, gave me this recipe. It was, he told me, his mother's. Even though I diminished the quantities considerably, this still makes a large loaf, sufficient for a good-sized party. Steam ½ pound of chicken livers just long enough to firm them. Grind them, along with ½ pound of fresh pork fat, 3 ounces of lean pork, and 3 anchovies, putting them through the grinder 3 times. Add 1 egg, ¾ teaspoon of salt, 1 cup of heavy cream, ½ cup of flour, ¼ teaspoon of thyme, and a little freshly ground black pepper. Mix well, then pour into a loaf pan that has been lined with thinly sliced bacon. Place in a pan of hot water and bake in a 350° oven for 1 hour. Serve with Melba toast.

SNAPS MED ØL: *A little glass of ice-cold Akvavit and a large glass of that superb Danish beer—a sort of Scandinavian boilermaker.*

141. *Gravad Lax*

A refreshing appetizer. . . . Have a 5- or 6-pound salmon filleted, but have the skin left on. Mix together ¼ cup of coarse salt (Kosher salt does nicely), a teaspoon of coarsely ground black pepper, 2 tablespoons of sugar, ¼ teaspoon of saltpetre, and either a half-dozen sprays of fresh dill or ¼ cup of dill weed. Spread this mixture on the cut sides of the fillets, put them together skin side out, and put a weighted board on top. Chill overnight. Next day slice on the diagonal, like smoked salmon, arrange on a plate, garnish with fresh dill. and accompany with wedges of lemon and buttered rye bread.

KENTUCKY MIST: *Fill an old-fashioned glass with shaved ice. Pour in Bourbon whiskey as desired, add a twist of lemon peel, and serve.*

142. Röktlax

Swedish smoked salmon balls, these, and mighty good eating. Combine a pound of finely ground smoked salmon, ½ pound of cream cheese, a teaspoon of lemon juice, a tablespoon of cream, and salt and pepper to taste. Roll in marbles, then in finely chopped fresh dill. Chill and serve on picks. (If you can't get fresh dill, use Spice Islands dill weed.)

CHAMPAGNE CUP: *This is a simple punch that is pleasantly dry. Sugar may be added, but we prefer it without. Combine a cup of sherry with the juice and zest of ½ lemon and 5 thin slices of unpeeled cucumber. Let this mixture stand for several hours, then combine with 2 bottles of chilled Champagne and pour the punch over ice.*

143. *Guacamole*

This has become almost as well-known as mayonnaise, but I include a recipe just in case. Mash 2 very ripe avocados and combine with ¼ cup of grated onion, a chopped canned green chile (or a teaspoon of chili powder), a tablespoon of lemon juice, and salt to taste. A peeled, seeded, and chopped tomato may be added, too. This turns dark if allowed to stand too long, so it is a good idea to float the lemon juice on top and beat it in just before serving.

TEQUILA DAISY: *Shake vigorously with ice: 4 ounces of tequila, and 1 ounce each of lemon juice, grenadine, and charged water. Strain into chilled cocktail glasses. You may add sugar if you like, but grenadine is pretty sweet.*

144. *Spicy Onion Rings*

Everyone goes for French fried onions, but when they're puffed and spicy besides, you'd better plan on twice as many as you think you'll need. Slice sweet onions—Italian, Spanish or Bermuda—¼-inch thick and divide into rings. Cover with milk and soak overnight. In the morning, drain, dip in seasoned flour, again dip in the milk, and again in the flour. (For each cup of flour add 1 teaspoon of salt, some freshly ground black pepper, and 2 teaspoons of curry powder or chili powder.) Fry the onions in deep fat at 375° until very lightly browned. Drain on paper. Just before serving with cocktails, fry again in fat at 400° until brown and puffy.

COLUMBIAN COOLER: *Fill thin lemonade glass ⅓ full of fine ice, 1 jigger Jamaica rum, ½ jigger Crème de Menthe; stir gently, fill with ice, serve with straws*
—"Mixed Drinks, Up to Date," 1895

145. *Chicken in Paper*

Entrancing, this Chinese dish, but best served out-of-doors or at a very informal gathering, along with hot towels. Cut raw breast of chicken in pieces about 1 inch square, ½-inch thick. Marinate them in a mixture of ¼ cup each of soy sauce and sherry, and 1 tablespoon of cooking oil, plus a crushed clove of garlic and 2 teaspoons of slivered green or candied ginger. Put a piece of chicken in the middle of a 5-inch square of parchment paper, bond paper, or foil, and top chicken with a tiny wisp of Chinese parsley (also known as fresh coriander or *cilantro*). Fold bottom of paper up over chicken, fold sides in, then tuck top into bottom, securing it between the first fold and the two side folds. When ready to serve, fry in deep fat for 2 minutes and serve in the paper.*

*HOT TOWELS: *Terry cloth fingertip towels, or napkins, wrung out in hot water and rolled tight to keep warm, are blessed by guests with sticky or greasy fingers!*

INDEX